★ ★ ★ ★ ★ ★ ★

Special Forces
FOR A
Special People

★ ★ ★ ★ ★ ★ ★ ★ ★ ★ ★ ★ ★

DWIGHT HALL

REMNANT PUBLICATIONS
COLDWATER, MICHIGAN

Published by Remnant Publications, Inc.
649 E. Chicago Rd.
Coldwater, MI 49036
www.remnantpublications.com

Edited by Ken McFarland
Page composition by Page One Communications
Cover design by David Berthiaume

ISBN 978-1-933291-37-6

Contents

Dedication

I dedicate this book first to my family, who has helped me in my personal struggles. It took me a long time to realize that the friction we make with one another—if understood as the all-knowing God of the universe does—will only make us wiser and better. I found out that we are on the same team.

Second, I want to dedicate this book to my coworkers. As we learn how special we truly are, we learn that we can make a difference, not only with our workplace, but we can even affect the world.

Last, but certainly not least, I dedicate this precious book to you, the reader. Never let anyone tell you that you are not special. There is only one of you—no matter how many times you have messed up. Remember this: You are only a failure when you quit. NEVER—and I mean NEVER—give up!! God will see us through.

Preface

Y ou're not famous—not a household name. You're not on the big screen—or the small one. You don't have to run from the cameras when you're in public. Your phone doesn't ring night and day with reporters wanting to interview you. You haven't set records in golf, football, or track.

You're just . . . ordinary.

You live a fairly uneventful life. But sometimes, you dream . . .

- ▶ Have you ever wished that your life could *really count* for something?
- ▶ Have you ever wished you could really *be somebody?*
- ▶ Have you ever wished you could just once do something *extraordinary*—maybe even heroic?

If so, I want you to know before you read even one more sentence— you *can* be someone special. You can do something as heroic as any person ever has in all history. You can be a part of something grand, magnificent—even breathtaking. And you need to understand that I'm not just blowing smoke. I could not be more serious.

A few pages from now, I'm going to share my own experience,

when as a young man, I became part of the Army Special Forces unit called the Airborne Rangers—an elite, highly trained, highly disciplined military regiment. But my message to you in this book is that I've been called again for the greatest Special Forces assignment yet—and I'm asking you to join me.

The United States Army, Navy, Air Force, Marines, and Coast Guard divisions comprise together the greatest military force this world has ever known. Within these branches of the service are the "few and the proud"—the elite, the best of the best—the various units known together as "Special Forces." These include many units, perhaps the best-known of which are the Army Green Berets, Rangers, and Delta Force; the Navy SEALs; and the U.S. Special Operations Command—which coordinates specialized operations across most of the military branches.

As a young man, I visited an Army recruiter before joining the service. But in this book I'm coming to you in an urgent attempt to recruit *you* into the greatest Special Forces unit ever assembled on this earth—as it prepares for the final battle in the greatest war ever fought in the history of Earth.

Uncle Sam isn't calling you. The president isn't calling you. I'm not even calling you. *God is!*

But, you might say, "I didn't even pass my Physical Training test in school. I could never make it." My answer is you've already started by just getting this book. No matter what your background is, you can make it. Failure is not an option! Hang in there, trainee! Only if you quit, do you fail. You might say, "But I am so weak in almost everything." Great! The Bible says that through your weaknesses you will be STRONG in Jesus.

You want your life to matter? You want to be part of something important?

Then join me in a Special Forces unit far more significant than the Army Rangers. I'll share with you my own story—and then the urgent need God has for volunteers to take on the most demanding assignment He's ever given to human beings.

God needs you!

✩ CHAPTER ONE ✩

"I Am Going to Kill Myself"

I could not believe it. I wanted to disappear. How could this have happened to me? What would happen to me now? I have to face my parents," I thought. "But I can't. I won't! I just want to kill myself."

As I changed my clothes in my dorm room, I thought that surely, I had to be dreaming. I blinked, but the same picture came to mind. I'd just been in the dean's office, and his words were still burning in my ears:

"Dwight, we have reason to believe you have been taking drugs. We are going to take you to the hospital and get you tested. I want you to sit right here while I call your parents."

"No!"—my mind was screaming. Not now. Not my parents. But the next words I heard were, "Mrs. Hall, we believe your son Dwight has been taking drugs, and we want to take him to the hospital to have a drug test done. We need your permission to do this."

All I could think was, "It's over. I am through. I am a failure. I will never be anything but a no-good bum." If my parents were as smart as I thought they were, they should just tell me not to come home. I mean, why should I embarrass them anymore?

All these thoughts and others ripped through my mind at supersonic speed. Breaking into my disastrous thoughts, I heard my mother through the phone, asking, "Is my son able to talk to me?"

"I want to talk to my mom!" I instantly yelled out. The dean handed over the phone.

"Mom, it is not as bad as you think. I'm fine."

Mom was undoubtedly shook up—and rightfully so. I heard the dean breaking into our conversation, saying, "You need to get off the phone—this is long distance, you know."

"Mom," I said. "The dean is complaining about the cost of the phone call. I will call you right back. Is that OK," I asked the dean.

"Yes," he said.

I hung up the phone and started to redial to make the collect call, when the dean's words shot through me like a bullet.

"Dwight, go get changed. We are going to the hospital. You can call your mom later."

"But you said I could call her back," I protested.

"And you will—but not this minute. Now go change."

Now I was feeling not only like a failure—but I was mad.

"Sure," I grumbled, as I strode out of his office and up the stairs to my room. And now as I started to change my clothes, it all came back to me like a recurring nightmare…

I had started the year with great intentions. This was my junior year, so I was an upper classman. Eleventh grade—only one more year. I had taken extra credits to maybe even graduate my junior year from the boarding academy I attended. I had been there since my freshman year. My grades averaged around a 2.0 (C). Everyone—or at least it seemed that way—told me that if I would only apply myself, I could and would do better. So this year was the year. It went well for a while, but then I lost focus.

A couple of friends of mine asked me to meet them in the woods to do something totally cool. I was always up for a challenge. When I got out there, they lit up a joint. "Wow," I thought, Should I do this? What would they think if I said No?" I was cool—or at least I thought I was. I took it and said to myself, "Now, this is something—smoking marijuana at a Christian academy."

Some weeks later, back in my room, I decided I would change my life. I started to have prayer with a few guys who came to my room. I buckled down and started for the first time in years to get good grades. Things seemed to be going so well—and then it happened. While I sat in one of my classes, a student came into the room and said, "The principal wants to see you."

What could this be about? I asked myself. I will never forget that when I said that, the impression distinctly came to me that it could be about smoking pot that one time about two months earlier.

No, I instantly stomped that thought out of my mind, there is just no way—it has been too long. It has to be something else. But to my utter dismay, the words came at me like an out-of-control freight train.

"Dwight, I heard that you were smoking marijuana. Is that true?"

My first thought was to lie. I reasoned with myself, "It's been two months ago. They can't prove anything." Yet, my dad had always and sometimes painfully taught me to tell the truth. I can still hear those words: "Dwight, no matter what—never lie. Take your punishment, even if you can get away with it. Once you go there, people will never know when or whether you are telling the truth."

So without much hesitation, I said, "That's true. But that was two months ago, and now I am doing so well." So, before the day was out, they sent me home with all my belongings.

I went home and felt *so* humiliated. Weeks passed. By then, my parents put me in our local public school, and for the next nine weeks, I went through the motions. At the end of December, one of my friends who had also been kicked out called me.

"Hey, Dwight," he said, "I am up here at Cedar Lake. You need to see if your parents will let you come up here." "Never, I thought. My dad had emphatically said, "You will stay here, where we can keep an eye on you. No more being away from home."

As the days went by, I could not get my friends out of my mind. I prayed to God and said, "Lord, if You will soften my parents' attitude so they will let me go, I will honor You."

I waited for the appropriate time when it seemed as if my parents were in a good mood—and hit them with the question.

"Mom and Dad," I began, "I have been going to our high school for the last nine weeks, and it has been OK, but I want to go back and get a Christian education. I have learned my lesson, and I promise—cross my heart and hope to die promise—that I will be one of the best students up there."

After what seemed like an eternity, they finally said Yes. I was so excited, I couldn't wait to call my friends.

So, starting in January with the new semester, I was off to another school—my third in less than twelve weeks. When I got there, I read my Bible every night. I tried to do the best I could, but my friends had not really changed. I also met new friends, and it seemed as if I always chose friends who were on the edge. Within six weeks I was back to my old habits.

I had always wanted to be special. We all do. God puts that desire into our minds because He makes each of us unique. I mean, right down to our own set of fingerprints. My problem was that Satan had little by little stolen my mind and good eyesight. He had perverted the word *special*, so it became the phrase, "Let's fit in." I had taken the bait—hook, line, and sinker.

Look at me, I thought, as I finished tying my shoes. Back to my room after that tense scene in the dean's office, I found my thoughts tumbling over each other. "I am nothing but a failure," I thought. "Wait till the church finds out about *this* at home; I will be a laughingstock. And what about my parents? What will they have to go through? If I were them, I wouldn't even go to that church anymore. I could hear it now: 'What's wrong with your son, Darwin?' . . . 'Joyce, did you ever train him to behave at home?'"

My thoughts became as heavy as a ton of bricks. "Special. You're right," I thought. "I am special—a special, no-good failure. I will never be anything." Right then and there I said to myself," I am not going home. I would rather kill myself."

I went to the window and saw one of the students who lived in town and had his own car. I opened the window and said, "Hey, I need a lift. Would you take me to town?"

"No problem," came the anticipated answer. I threw some clothes together, grabbed some of my most important belongings, and headed out the fire escape door. Once in the car, I thought, I really am running away. This is it—no turning back now. What's the use, anyway? I can't do anything right. I am just a failure. No, I am a special failure—I mean bad!

"Where in town do you want to go?"

I heard the question through my fractured thoughts.

"I need to get to a phone," I said.

"Well, there is a phone booth in town by the gas station."

"Great," I said.

"What then?" he countered.

"I don't know," I replied, "but I will figure it out."

I at least had to let my mom know why I had not called her right back. After getting out of the car and stepping into the phone booth, I stuck my hands into my pockets, and wouldn't you know—there was not even a penny.

"Great," I said to myself," I don't even have enough to pay for a call." Once again, like a baseball bat slamming into me, the words blasted through my mind, "You're a mess. Nothing but one big hiccup. Dwight, with you, failure is just the beginning. At the rate you're going, they don't even have a word to describe you."

I still needed to call mom, I thought. She will be worried sick. It had been almost an hour since I last talked to her, and I had told her I would call right back. That was the least I could do for her. One of these days I would pay her back for the phone call.

"Hello—yes, operator, I would like to make a collect call. Yes, that number is correct."

"Hi, Mom . . ."

And what met my ears next, I will never forget. My mother was sobbing. I could tell that she was trying to control herself, and just as I was thinking, "You just messed up again," I heard her say, "Dwight, wherever you are, stay there, and I will pick you up."

"Mom, I have decided to run away. I don't deserve you or Dad. I am just one big mess-up."

"Dwight," Mom said, "we have all made mistakes. Dad and I will never give up on you. We all make mistakes. Please—I beg you—stay there, and I will come and pick you up."

"Mom, you're just trying to be nice. Besides, even if you are telling me the truth, I know Dad doesn't think so." As I was saying this, I was glad my father was at that time in Florida, building apartments. It was amazing to me as I recalled that Dad was also in Florida when I got kicked out the last time. I was sure that he would have punished me to within an inch of my life. To think that Dad only went twice to Florida—and those two times were when I got kicked out!

Jarred out of my thoughts again, I heard Mom say, "Dwight, you know that is not true. Dad won't be happy, but he knows as well as I do that we all make mistakes. Dwight, you are special to us."

"Special," I thought again. "Yeah, right." Then my mother was crying again, and she said, "Please, Dwight, promise me you will stay there. I love you very much."

Then I was crying. "I can't even hang tough," I thought. What a sissy. I can't even run away right. But those three power-packed phrases that Mom had just said sparked me to life:

"Dad and I will never give up on you."

"Dwight, you are special to us."

"I love you very much."

In the end, I did stay there. It was one of the best decisions I ever made.

I wish I could say that I went home and lived happily ever after, but that is far from the truth. My life's journey had only begun. As I sat there and waited for Mom to arrive, I wondered so very slightly, "Was it really possible to be special? How would I ever get there? Was there anybody out there who finally became famous or special who had messed up their lives as much as I had?"

Special. Not a hard word—but so mystical. Almost like a mirage, you can see it—but when you go to grasp it, it turns out to be nothing but desert sand.

Where was I going to go from here? What will Dad do to me when he gets back from Florida? What will he say? Where will I go to school?

I would just have to wait and see.

THE BOTTOM LINE:

1. In a world of 6.6 billion people, the desire of each one of us to be special—to somehow be unique and different—to matter is universal.

2. What does being special mean to you? Having value to someone? Having unique abilities? Becoming known for what you do or accomplish?

3. Does "messing up" or making mistakes mean you are not special?

CHAPTER TWO

To Be Somebody

As I look back, I can truly see—just as clearly as I can see the chair I am sitting on right now—how God was directing my life for the good. God never intended for me to mess up as I did years ago. But He is so loving that He does not force us to do right. He loves us so much that He gives us free will—the power of free choice. This tells me every day, like a screaming siren, that I am *special* to Him.

Back to my story...I was so thankful that my dad and I would both have some time before we would see each other. During that time at home, not being in school, I had a lot of time to think.

What had gotten me into this nasty position? How could I utterly mess up twice in such a short time? I went back in my life many years to try and find the beginnings of my failures that had accumulated to bring me where I was at this point. I found two main clues. One is what I call "playing church." The other was caring too much what other people thought—especially my friends. Was I willing to give God my all, even if they made fun of me, even if I felt enormous peer pressure against going all the way with Him?

So let me take you back to my life as a young man living in Michigan. I grew up in a Christian home and worked for my father and uncle in construction. But though I'd grown up in the church, like most young people, I arrived at a time in my life when I began questioning everything, including my faith.

I'd go to church, and it seemed as if the people were the same when I was 18 years of age as they had been when I was little. Some of those adults had been going to church for forty or fifty years, but it seemed to me as if they were just going through the motions—that nothing had changed for them. I couldn't know their hearts, of course, but it seemed to me as if they were mostly just playing church—living in denial and just "pretending" at being Christians.

I saw two completely opposite kinds of Christians.

On the one hand were those whose way of "playing church" seemed to focus on keeping all the rules. The more rules one kept, the better Christian he or she was. Now, I know as a Christian that there are do's and don'ts. The Bible is full of rights and wrongs. We just cannot get away from them, and we shouldn't even want to. God has given us a set of rules— commandments—for guidance. It's because of His love that He gave these commandments to us.

I want to say right here that I am not against rules. We need them. But when we keep them—or try to—just to impress others or to make others look bad because they don't keep them, we become legalists. Even more than this, I have seen so many people keeping those rules and not enjoying it one bit. It's as if they are saying, "I will keep these rules even if it kills me." The bottom line is that it's superficial if it is not from the heart.

The problem was that I did not see the lives of the Christians I knew reflecting Jesus. In other words, it seemed to me that they could be going to church every weekend, giving Bible studies, and even holding church offices, but in private or away from church, they were anything but Christian in how they lived.

The other kind of Christian to me was just as bad. I call it the "feels good religion." They go to church when they feel like it. They claim Jesus as their personal Savior, sing praise songs with all kinds of feeling, and wear all kinds of pins and other outward showy things. I have seen many of them get what I call an emotional high. It's almost like being on some kind of drug. I know, I've been there. Those people just drifted aimlessly not doing much of anything—just claiming to be Christians while going out and having a "good time" and living as they pleased. Live and let live, seemed to be their philosophy. Jesus is my Savior—which is good—so that gives me the right to live any way I want. Forget the rules. I am saved anyway. I will accept His gift—His blood—but Lord of my life, NO WAY. To me, it was all a facade. Playing church!

Playing Church?

I remember a friend telling me a story about a pilot who showed him his beautiful airplane. It had all the latest avionics. This pilot was showing him all the fancy things his plane could do and how all the avionics worked. At the end, my friend said these astounding words, "You have thoroughly convinced me that this plane has the latest and greatest tools to get you through pretty much anything. But I want to know just one thing."

"What's that?" the pilot asked.

"Can you fly the plane?"

The thought that kept coming through loud and clear to me was—talk is cheap. I did not want to hear about it anymore. So you can talk the talk. Can you walk the walk? Or are you just playing church?

As a young man, I wanted something solid—something that really had meaning. I also wanted three things nearly every young person wants:

▶ I wanted freedom.
▶ I wanted to fit in.
▶ I wanted to be somebody.

My high school years, as I described in the previous chapter, were really stormy. In my junior year, I was kicked out of one Christian high school, spent a brief time at a local public high school, then enrolled in another Christian high school, from which I was soon kicked out as well.

I came out of this time disillusioned, bitter, and ready to just throw everything over and go the way of the world. Inside, I really hungered for a genuine, fully committed Christian experience—but some of my school teachers had shown me just too much hypocrisy and had treated me in ways that were decidedly unchristian. The kind of experience for which I hungered, I hadn't seen demonstrated by those I thought should know how to have it—and I began to lose hope that it even existed.

So what became the most important, driving force in my whole life now was this: I wanted to be somebody. I was determined that I would not fail again.

Along with working with my dad in construction, unknown to anyone else, I was taking flying lessons at the local airport during my lunch hour each day. One day, the instructor didn't show up, or the weather wasn't the best—I don't remember just which. Having some time to kill, I walked down a street in my little town of Coldwater, Michigan, and I saw a sign right above me that said, "Army Recruiting Office."

Join Up? Me? Never!

Let me tell you that I'd never had any interest in joining the military. In fact, I had always said to myself that I would never, ever join. I thought that people who did were stupid. Yes, if I were drafted, I'd serve—but join? Never!

So I went in, and the recruiting sergeant asked what he could do for me.

"Oh, nothing," I replied. "I'm just killing some time."

The recruiter on duty that day was no dummy. He asked me what I wanted to do in life. So I told him. I wanted to learn to fly, to travel, to avoid college, to make good money, and to have a really good time—that's what. I even told him I wanted to be somebody.

The recruiter had heard all he needed—and he knew just what buttons to push.

"You can do all of that, and more, in the Army," he said.

My eyes widened. He had my full attention then, and he knew it.

"Listen," he started. "If there's anything you could do that you'd most enjoy, what would it be?"

"I'll tell you what," I answered. "What I'd like to do is be a truckdriver in Hawaii. If you could get me a job as a truckdriver in Hawaii, then hey, I'd join up."

Of course, I knew I was safe with such a specific request. No way could he make that happen. Still, what a dream job! My head filled with visions of learning to surf while surrounded by legions of beautiful, tanned women—then just bumming out on the beach on weekends. What a life!

The next day, the recruiter called me. "Now, listen," he said, "everyone who joins the service has to take a physical and a written exam. But if you go to Detroit and take those tests and pass, I've got you right now lined up to drive a military truck in Hawaii."

"You've got to be kidding me!" I said.

So I told my parents, certain they would be ecstatic. Hardly. It was like, "Here we go again with Dwight." They were deeply disappointed. Among other things, they feared for my spiritual welfare in the service. I wasn't living a Christian life as it was, and in the Army, they thought things could get even worse. They just didn't understand why I hadn't discussed this issue with them.

They explained the principle to me that one mind is not sufficient to make big decisions. Even God who created us gave us this counsel in His Word. How important those words of wisdom were. "Iron sharpeneth iron; so a man sharpeneth the countenance of his friend" (Proverbs 27:17). "In the multitude of counselors there is safety" (Proverbs 11:14; 13:10; 15:22).

But my parents' reservations didn't dim my enthusiasm in the least, and about a month later I went to Detroit and took the two tests. The written test took quite a while, and when I was done, I waited with several others until a man in a really sharp uniform stepped out and said, "Hall?"

He took me into an office and told me to take a seat.

"Dwight," he said, "you passed both tests with flying colors." This was music to my ears, especially after the accumulation of failures still fresh in my mind from high school. "In fact," he continued, "you did so well on the written exam that I have an offer to make you."

"And what's that?" I asked.

"There's a very special unit of the Army called the Airborne Rangers," he said. "We pull into the Rangers only those who show exceptional promise and potential." He paused meaningfully before delivering the punch line: "We have just a few openings for a few select men."

"Really?" I sat up straight in my chair and looked the recruiter eye to eye.

"These are tough units." he went on. "The one I'd like to put you in is the Airborne Rangers, which is kind of like the Green Berets. You say you'd like to fly?"

"Yes, sir!" I could hardly stay in my chair.

"Well, the Airborne Rangers get to jump out of airplanes." He continued, "They wear a black beret, and because of their bravery, they are the first ones to go into battle."

The recruiter pulled out a picture of a solidly muscled Ranger and leaned forward earnestly, eyeing my slender frame.

"Do you see this picture, Dwight?"

"Yes, sir."

"Well, when the Airborne Rangers get done with you, your

body will look like this. We're in the business of turning men just like you into lean, mean fighting machines."

It would have taken a battalion of Rangers to keep me *out* of this elite unit! This man had said I'd be special. He'd said they would make me lean and mean. This last promise especially hit home with me. Back in school, the girls used to comment about how skinny I was.

"You have a really cute smile, Dwight," was one of their favorite lines, "but unfortunately, when you turn sideways you disappear."

The decision to be an Airborne Ranger instead of a truckdriver in Hawaii was a no-brainer for me. Sure, I wanted to have fun in the sun and travel. But I could do that as a Ranger too. Best of all, as an Airborne Ranger I would finally be somebody. I'd be needed. I'd be special. I'd be part of something awesomely important. It would be worth the blood, sweat, and tears. I would play a part to help protect my country. I loved my country. I believed that there would be no superficial people in the military. I couldn't sign fast enough. I'd have paid him to get in!

THE DESIRE GOD PUTS IN US ALL

Let me just say here that this desire to be somebody—to feel needed and important—is in all of us. We all want to belong—to fit in. And it's not a bad thing. God made us this way. And at this point in my life, the military seemed to hold my best promise for finally being somebody.

Now I could hardly wait to tell my parents and friends all about it as soon as I got home.

"I'm going to be an Airborne Ranger." I told them. "I will be part of an elite unit in the Army, where they only have room for a few good men."

If my parents had been apprehensive about my decision to join the military, after I told them I intended to join the Rangers, they were nearly beside themselves—especially when I told them that

Rangers were first into battle and had a short life expectancy in combat. Of course, I was young, so like most young people, I just knew I was invincible and would never die. I felt bulletproof.

I'd made enough from my construction work to buy a sleek black Cobra, and it couldn't run the Coldwater streets fast enough as I sped down to the recruiting office, anxious to tell the officer of my good fortune. I knew without a doubt that he, at least, would be delighted for me.

"You have got to be kidding me!" he gasped, shaking his head. "When the Airborne Rangers go into battle, they have the shortest life expectancy of anybody."

In an effort to dissuade me from my decision, he showed me a movie of Airborne Rangers in action—in all kinds of dangerous situations.

"Now what do you think, Dwight?" he said when the movie ended, certain that it had scared me witless.

"Man, I can't wait to get in there!" I told him.

The recruiter could only shake his head, knowing I had to be crazy.

While I was surprised at his response, the recruiting officer's cautionary words didn't faze me one bit. In fact, the idea of defying death excited me all the more. I would get to fly. I would get to travel. There would fun and adventure. And most importantly of all—at last, *I would be somebody.*

I took the tests in the fall of 1974 and didn't have to report for training until January of 1975, so I had a few months to get myself ready for this new chapter in my life. "What would it be like?" I kept wondering. My nights were filled with dreams of impossible feats. "Would I make it? Could I hang in there?" One thing I kept repeating over and over to myself was that I would die trying.

THE BOTTOM LINE:

1. What were the two kinds of Christians I saw while growing up?

2. What was the driving desire of my life as a young man? What is this desire God has put in us all?

3. What fear led my parents to be less than enthusiastic when I shared with them the news that I had signed up to join the Army?

✪ CHAPTER THREE ✪

Basic Training: Fort Polk, Louisiana

As 1975 began, I reported to Fort Polk, Louisiana, to start basic training toward becoming a part of the elite 75th Ranger Regiment—the premier raid force of the U.S. Army.

The Army has many posts where basic training is conducted. Fort Polk specialized in those being trained for the Infantry and for various Special Forces assignments—primarily the Green Berets and the Airborne Rangers. I can't speak for just how these two elite units function today, but back then, the Green Berets seemed more involved with specialized intelligence training, while the Rangers took on more front-line combat operations. Still, there was some crossover between the units.

Orientation at Fort Polk took about two days before we started our basic training in earnest. We were shown our barracks, got our shots and uniforms and dog tags—and of course, were shorn of our hair like sheep. I watched as the guy next to me was sheared of his locks, and I began to laugh and couldn't stop.

But when my own carefully tended shoulder-length hair fell to the floor and I looked in the mirror, my laughter stopped. As long as I'd be around my fellow soldiers, and all of us had buzz cuts, I'd be fine. But I knew that on leave, back in the big, wide civilian world, I was headed for some really uncomfortable, self-conscious moments. As a young man, my hair was an important part of my image. If a guy had short hair in those days, they would say, "Hey, man—you look like a goonhead retard!"—or worse.

What would people think of me when I went back home? I quickly put some positive thoughts into my mind: "It's OK, Dwight. It doesn't matter what they think, because you're special. You will be an Airborne Ranger, and you can handle anything! Let them think what they want. You know what you are, and no amount of nasty words or backbiting will change you."

Once orientation was done, they loaded us onto "cattle trucks"— each carrying fifty or sixty of us with all our belongings jammed into our duffle bags—and drove us to another part of the base where our basic training would begin.

When we arrived and began to unload, we were met by some mean-looking drill sergeants. But they reassuringly told us to take our time. Each of the companies in our battalion had maybe a hundred men—and two or three drill sergeants were assigned to each company.

I was in Charlie Company—and our drill sergeant was a big African American soldier named Sergeant Sibley. He too told us to just take our time unloading and settling into our new barracks.

No More Mister Nice Guy

But about halfway to the barracks, drill sergeant Sibley seemed to suffer an abrupt and total personality change. He began shouting and screaming at us. Right up close, he'd yell into our ears, cursing and ordering us to hurry up. Sergeant Sibley transformed in an instant from a Nice Guy into a Tyrant. For weeks now, he'd be in our faces around the clock.

I had some foggy idea going in that basic training would be tough, but I was really clueless as to just how tough it would be.

What I would later understand was that the Army had to strip us of all self-will so that we were prepared to respond instantly and without question to authority—to orders—and then it could begin to build us back up into the fighting men it needed.

Two or three weeks into basic training, Sibley taught us to chant in unison, "Hot stuff, drill sergeant—hot stuff. Second by name . . . first by fame. Hot stuff, drill sergeant—hot stuff!"

We were the second of the four platoons in Charlie Company— "second by name." But when our training performance was outstanding, Sibley would order us to sound off and chant the "hot stuff" mantra. It's hard to describe the pride we felt in those moments. We knew we had done well!

Life in the Airborne Rangers was tougher than tough, but I rose to the challenge. Our superiors focused on one goal—preparing their charges for battle—and they did a good job of it.

Physically, we engaged in constant marches, maneuvers, and workouts, like jumping off a three-foot wall when we were in jump school over and over again. We had to land just right and then get up in the next breath. If we didn't, a sergeant yelled in our ears and kicked sawdust in our faces.

The Airborne Rangers worked on our minds too. We had to focus every inch of our being on an enemy, hate that enemy, and want to kill that enemy. In the 1970s, the Communists were the "enemy of choice." I remember sitting in the Army bleachers with fifty or more guys, with the sergeant yelling, "Who wants to kill a commie today?" And we would all shout. "I do! I do! I do!" And we did that over and over again.

We had no free time. No privacy. Our days were filled with grueling physical training, to which was added frequent discipline in the form of pushups for most any infraction—whether intentional or not.

At times during basic training, I wondered if I could take it—or have to wash out. But then I'd look around at my fellow trainees and say to myself, "If they can do it, Dwight—you can do it." Ultimately, a few did wash out, but I think I had at least one advantage, other than my overwhelming desire to finish this and be somebody. I'd learned discipline, hard work, and obedience from my dad. I hadn't always seen these qualities as anything good—but here, they really did help.

This background also stood me in good stead when, by the luck of the alphabet, I was chosen as leader of my squad of ten men.

Basic training was so tough that when it was finished, only seven soldiers out of more than a hundred got their private stripes (or "mosquito wings," as we called them). I was proud to be in that number.

AIT Training

The next "step up" the training ladder was Advanced Individualized Training, or AIT. After a week of leave following the eight-week basic training course, I was due right back at Fort Polk to begin AIT, which would go for another eight weeks.

AIT took us into expert training in hand-to-hand combat, weapons handling and assembly/disassembly, proficiency in use of mortars and Claymore mines, night-combat skills, and much more. In advanced training, we also received a few more privileges—more free time, no more marching to the mess hall, etc.

In some ways, AIT made basic training look easy, but once again I rose to the challenge. I wanted to turn my body into that "lean, mean fighting machine"—to be successful in something I did—to be somebody. When AIT was over, once again I stood proudly among the few first-time "achievers," being one of just seven to receive my PFC (Private First Class) stripes.

Jump School: Fort Benning, Georgia

The final step of my training for the Rangers was the three-week Airborne Ranger Jump School. I could not become a Ranger without being airborne-qualified.

Summertime in Georgia was miserable. In full combat gear, we trained in hot, muggy conditions that were nearly unbearable. To add to my absolute misery, I had picked up a roaring case of poison ivy while still in AIT in Fort Polk. In the heat and humidity of Georgia, it now spread like wildfire to probably 80 percent of my body. My skin grew raw—and a visit to the Army physician really didn't get me much help. I would wake up in the middle of the night with blood on my sheets and skin under my fingernails, because I had unknowingly been scratching myself. My skin was raw from all that scratching.

But I dared not take time out from my training. The rule was that if anyone missed even one hour of training, he flunked. I was too determined to let that happen.

Each new step of my training was a step higher in difficulty. In jump school, I wasn't even called by my name. We were called by our roster numbers. I was #62. Jump school included officers as well as those of us who were non-commissioned. It included Navy SEALs as well as those training to be Rangers. But in jump school, we were all on an equal footing. Rank didn't count.

Our drill sergeants weren't called that in jump school but were known as "black caps" for the caps they wore. And I could tell that some of our black caps of lower rank took particular pleasure in making life difficult for the officers they trained.

On the day of my final jump, I had a fever of about 104 degrees from the poison ivy and the physical demands of the training. I was so out of it, it's a wonder I made it. I felt as if I might pass out. It's one of the toughest things I've ever done.

But I passed. And I was in the top five of my class. Finally, I was on my way to being a very special person. Now I would be assigned to the 75th Ranger Battalion. I couldn't wait. What would it be like? Would my dream be finally realized?

I was about to find out.

THE BOTTOM LINE:

1. What part of preparation for basic training made me most self-conscious and apprehensive?

2. What percentage of new recruits made it through basic training?

3. What miserable physical challenge tested my resolve during jump school? What kept me going?

CHAPTER FOUR

Dwight Hall— Army Ranger

Now at last, I was an Army Ranger—no longer a trainee—though training in some form continues as long as one is in the military. In Fort Lewis, Washington, I was issued my Ranger black beret, my camouflage fatigues (no longer the olive drab of a trainee), and my Class-A Ranger dress uniform.

We might be Rangers, but we still faced ongoing training—and in Fort Lewis, we specialized in night-time maneuvers. Georgia had been hot, now Fort Lewis was cold and rainy. We could not wear raincoats—too noisy. We could not build campfires. After all, we were practicing ambush tactics.

We'd lie on the ground soaked to the skin, shivering uncontrollably in the cold forests of Washington state. I recalled visions of clean, dry, warm white sheets, and I promised myself to find some when I was finished with all this.

I had come a long way from that day in Coldwater when I stopped at the recruiting office. I'd been recruited into the Rangers, gone through basic training, advanced training, jump school, and now my permanent assignment at Fort Lewis.

I wish I could say all this made me happy, but I can't. There was a nagging emptiness in my heart—a void I tried in vain to fill by being a model soldier.

While I was in the Airborne Rangers, I continued to attend church when I could. In my own way, I even tried to keep the Sabbath. If my unit marched over to the camp store, I went along but I wouldn't buy anything because it was Sabbath.

Clinging to some of my childhood convictions didn't keep me from drinking, however. It seemed as though everyone in the service drank—and drank heavily. There wasn't much else to do in the evenings, and since being a model soldier hadn't taken away the void in my life, I tried to fill it with drinking. While I never got heavily into hard liquor or drugs, I drank beer by the case. In addition, I frequented some places I am now ashamed to mention.

Night after night, I staggered back to the barracks, drunk. But somehow, maybe from force of habit, I knelt by my bed to pray. But because I knew that God would hear a sincere prayer, I also knew He would be the only one who could take care of my burden, the burden of guilt. He alone, I could trust.

I wanted to surrender to Him, but I didn't know how. Other people said they had surrendered, but their actions did not show the precious victory I longed to experience. So there by my bunk, I would bury my face in the green wool army blanket and talk to God.

In my heart I knew that something was drastically wrong—that I wasn't happy and that something vitally important was missing from my life. My prayers began like this: "Lord, I know I'm going to hell." And I was sure of it, for the Bible said that "the wages of sin is death" (Romans 6:23). I knew I was living a life of sin, but I also didn't want to be a hypocrite. I figured if I was going to hell, at least I would go honestly. I told God all of this and of my determination not to play church or be a pretender.

Sometimes, after a night out on the town when I was driving around in my little yellow truck, I would go find myself a quiet road and drive it. Then I would stop by a field and just sit there thinking—and look up at the stars.

"Is there really a God up there?" I would wonder to myself. "If there is, I hope He will help me straighten out my life." Although I wasn't acting on it, in my heart I had this desire to be a "real" Christian, whatever that was. I did know for sure a real Christian, and I mean real, would do what is right to be happy and have the peace the Bible talks about. I was slowly starting to see the true meaning of "special."

About this time I started getting frustrated with the Airborne Rangers. Earning my mosquito wings and becoming a PFC (one step higher than a private) so early in the game had taken away much of the challenge for me.

According to Army rules, I couldn't be promoted to sergeant until I had spent at least three years in the service. In the meantime, I was a subordinate to a group of other sergeants in the barracks. And when I say subordinate, I do mean I was in subordination to them. These guys took great pleasure in ordering the privates around. Whenever I passed them in the hall, which was quite frequently, they would make me stand at attention. And, in contrast to my feelings, they enjoyed every minute of it.

Then I started to think about what I had "accomplished" in the Airborne Rangers. True, I had been a model soldier. But I didn't get to do the things that were promised me when I enlisted. Other than jumping out of a few airplanes, I didn't get to fly. And except for being stationed in Seattle (which was a nice city but not exactly Hawaii) I didn't get to travel, either. And I spent a lot more time in the bars than I ever did on the beach.

I was unhappy, dissatisfied with my life. And I could see hypocrisy everywhere. A promise was one thing—but following through was something else. I just wanted real, live, honest people. I had accomplished my goal to be "somebody," but I certainly did not have the peace I wanted. So one night after being with my friends, drinking way too much, as usual, I got down on my knees, and started talking to God about it. I was quite drunk that night, but I asked God for three things:

▶ To get me out of the service early,

▶ To help me find a girl that would not like to party—that would love children, want to stay home and take care of them, and love being a wife to me, and

▶ To help me get to know Him—intimately know Him. I wanted a real experience with God.

"Lord, if You are out there, and if You are real, please show me," I prayed. "I want to walk with You.

"I've heard all about people like Elijah, Moses, John the Baptist, and Enoch in the Bible, Lord," I prayed. "But where are those people today? The people who put You first in everything—and I mean everything?"

In my heart, I desperately wanted to be a Christian. At the same time, I was determined not to be a hypocrite. And I certainly didn't want to be a fake. "God," I said, "if You are there, I know You would not be a hypocrite. I know You have do's and don'ts. But Lord, You are not superficial. You have put it into my heart to be special—to be somebody. Please help me, God. I am so afraid of failure."

So many times, I remember telling the Lord how unhappy I was, that I didn't want to live to just exist. As I looked around me, I saw people at every stage of life. Most were just going through the motions. When I looked at the older people who wouldn't be on planet Earth much longer, they seemed to have no hope of a better life.

"There's got to be more than this, God," I prayed. "Please help me."

Little did I realize that God would answer all three of my requests—though not all at the same time.

My first answer to prayer came when I received an early release from the service. Getting out of the Airborne Rangers into another branch of the service wasn't hard because the Rangers were a voluntary unit. All I had to do was tell my superior that I wanted out. Still, it was a struggle for me. In spite of my resolve, it seemed like throwing all my hard-earned accomplishments down the drain. In addition, quitting the Army early seemed like another failure to me. I wanted to finish what I had started.

In spite of these misgivings, I stuck to my decision and was soon transferred to a different unit. Once in my new unit, I managed to befriend the captain, and he really did seem to respect me. Part of it was that I was a "gung-ho" soldier. I was also very neat. All my uniforms were tailored exactly for my size. My shirts were starched, shoes spit-shined, and fatigues tapered to fit just right.

I can still remember the day I told the captain I wanted to quit. Not wanting to leave anything to chance, I thought through my speech carefully in advance—like playing a game of chess. I thought about what I would say and what the captain might say— and how I would respond.

When I finally got up my nerve, I marched into his office dressed in my finest uniform and stood at attention, as was the Army custom.

"Parade rest," The captain commanded. Then: "What's on your mind, Hall?"

"Sir, I want out of this man's army, Sir." I replied.

He was shocked at my request, and he didn't attempt to hide it. After all, I had been an all-out, highly committed soldier. At first, he didn't think I was really serious.

"Oh, that's great, Hall," he said sarcastically. "I want out of this man's army. Do you just think I will let you out?"

Fortunately, I had anticipated this reaction from him and even planned what I would say next.

"May I have permission to speak, Sir'?" I asked.

"Permission granted."

Then I explained my situation. That no matter how hard I worked, there was nothing left to achieve for another year and a half—that a year and a half seemed like a very long time to me—that this routine and being bossed around by all the sergeants seemed like worthless living to me—that life was too important for me to just "bum around" in the Army for another year.

"Well, what if we send you to school?" he inquired. "If you sign up for another four years, I'll send you to officer's training school."

I wasn't the least bit interested in that option.

"Sir, I don't want to sign up for another four years," I replied. "I just want out—now."

"What will you do?" The captain peppered me with questions. "Are you sure you can find a job?"

"I'm not worried about finding a job," I told him. "I know I can always work for my dad in construction."

In the end, the captain offered to call my dad and talk with him about the situation. This was unheard of in the Army, but he did it. Then he gave me a little advice.

"There's no reason for me to let you out of here, Hall," he said, "Although I suppose if you were to be a bad influence on the other soldiers, I would have to let you go." Then he said he could get me out, but it would have to be a general discharge under honorable conditions.

This was music to my ears. After all my hard work, I couldn't bear the thought of a dishonorable discharge. It was even hard on me to give up my starched and creased uniforms, but I decided to do it anyway. I wanted to make sure the captain had reason to let me out of the Army.

In the end, that didn't bother me. I was just so happy to be getting out—and a whole year early. During my days in the service I had kept in close contact with my parents. My mom flew out to Seattle to meet me. Together we loaded my few belongings into the yellow "Chevy Luv" truck I had bought out West and headed from Washington back to Michigan—and home.

I maybe didn't realize it at the time, but something became

clear to me in the years since my time in the Special Forces. In the Old Testament, the man Job also didn't realize what was really happening in his life for quite a while. But behind the scenes, God was working out His own chosen plan for Job's life.

One of the most powerful motivations driving my decision to join the Special Forces, as I've already shared, was the need to feel special. I needed to feel that I mattered—that I had value, that I could be a worthy man who could do worthwhile things.

And in the Special Forces, God helped me learn that lesson. But today I'm convinced that the reason I became restless in my military service was because God had more in mind for me than to spend my life in a military career.

At least, not in Uncle Sam's military!

When I had learned and come to understand that I indeed did matter—that I was indeed unique and special—God needed me out of the U.S. Army. He needed to maneuver me into the place He had waiting for me in HIS Army—His Special Forces!

It wouldn't be long after my discharge from the Rangers that God would tap me on the shoulder and invite me to accept the Special Forces assignment for Him that has consumed my life ever since.

THE BOTTOM LINE:

1. Even while drunk, I prayed for three things, and in time received them all. Do we have to stop all our sinning before God can hear and answer us?

2. Have you ever looked up into the night sky as I have and wondered if there really is a God up there? And if so, if He really cares about you?

3. Have you sometimes found it hard to trust that behind the scenes, God is working out His plan for your life?

CHAPTER FIVE

What Does It Mean to Be "Special"?

I felt good about myself. I had made it through some hard training. I had taken to heart what that recruiting officer had first told me after my physical.

"Remember, Dwight—you don't have to know anything. In fact, it's almost better that way. Just remember these three important things:

"Do what we tell you to do.

"Don't hesitate, trying to reason it out.

"And never give up—failure is not an option. You are only a failure when you quit."

Those words echoed through my mind hundreds of times, like the rumbling thunder of a massive thunderstorm. That was especially true at those times when I was more than a little apprehensive.

I remember the first time I jumped out of a perfectly good, safe airplane after all the ground training we did. My mind started talking to me.

"Dwight, hello—are you still there? Is anybody home? Have you gone completely nuts? Are you really going to jump out of this plane? What if your chute doesn't open? Have you ever thought about dying? Maybe you should start thinking about that right now!"

But I would stifle those negative thoughts, saying, "I will do what I've been told. I will not hesitate. And I will not quit, because failure is not an option."

Those three things proved to me to be a saving grace—they were indispensable.

As I have looked back on those exciting years and tried to put the pieces together. I've come up with the following:

1. We all want to be better than we currently are.

2. Being special is not just a familiar, well-used word. It has far more meaning than meets the common eye.

3. God's term *special* is greater and broader and deeper than our common view.

So let's take a moment to look a little more closely at those three statements.

We All Want to Be Better Than We Already Are

Think about it for a moment. The desire to be better, to be "more," to improve and grow, is just part of our being. How many times have you heard someone say—or perhaps you have said—"I can't believe I did such a lousy job! I could have done better." Or "I'll do better next time."

This desire and effort to become better is really part of our growth. In the Bible, when it refers to our spiritual growth—our character development—this process is called *sanctification*. We should be constantly learning and moving forward.

This is a fantastic privilege and awesome responsibility. If we are not, shame on us! Becoming better keeps us from being bored with life. It keeps us young—at least young in heart—and most importantly, it inspires others to do the same.

BEING SPECIAL HAS MUCH MORE MEANING THAN WE THINK

In the dictionary, the word *special* means "particular . . . distinct . . . unique . . .extraordinary . . . exceptional."

But *special* goes far beyond any dictionary definitions. When it comes to a truly special person—or someone in the Special Forces—special has to do with conviction, with commitment, with a total, single-minded focus on achieving something.

In some ways, of course, every human being ever born is special. Each one is unique. No two people have the same fingerprints, the same DNA, the same combination of physical or personality traits.

But there's a "special" that goes far beyond just being uniquely different from everybody else.

Would you say that it takes a special person to volunteer for a suicide mission? In most every war ever fought, that's happened. And it's not just one-of-a-kind fingerprints that drives a soldier to willingly volunteer to give up his life. That soldier has to really BELIEVE in something! And what he believes in has to be so important to him that it's bigger than himself. He has to value something more than he values himself.

In a war, it may be that a soldier volunteers for a mission from which he will never return because he is convinced that by doing so, he can defend his country and its freedoms from enemies determined to destroy it. He may voluntarily give up his life to save the lives of his comrades in arms. He may be thinking of his family back home—those he loves—and their protection calls from him the ultimate expression of his love for them. "Greater love has no man than this," the Bible says, "than to lay down his life for his friends" (John 15:13, NKJV).

Navy SEAL Danny Dietz did.

He gave his life for his friends.

In high school, Danny played football. But his real passion was martial arts—so he became an expert at using these skills.

"Danny was always training for something," his father recalled.

His dad remembered a day when, as part of Danny's never-ending training regimen, his lunch was largely raw oatmeal. Someone asked him what he planned to do after high school.

"Going to be a SEAL," Danny mumbled between chomps.

In late June of 2005, 25-year-old Navy SEAL Danny and his Special Forces teammates were patrolling a bleak Afghanistan mountainside when guerrilla gunfire shattered the quietness.

Bullets shredded trees, ricocheted off boulders, and one ripped into Dietz's body through eighty pounds of gear.

Gravely wounded, Danny fought for another twenty minutes, holding off and taking out many of the thirty or so guerrillas firing on his unit. In the end, only one of Danny's teammates survived—but that soldier credits Danny's heroic efforts with saving his life.

Do you see what I mean by "special"? A special person does something difficult, something extraordinary, something that seems impossible. And they don't have to force themselves to do it. They would have to force themselves NOT to do it.

A special person is totally motivated. That person is ready to put forth any effort, make any sacrifice, pay any price, to achieve his or her goal.

God's Term "Special" is Greater Than Our View

This is a principle so important to understand. Are you ready? Listen carefully to what I write next: **If the prize is high enough, the how becomes easier.**

Let me explain. Suppose you came to me and said, "Dwight, I need you to help me."

"No sweat," I say. "How can I help you?"

"I need you to deliver a package for me to Los Angeles."

"Is the package big or small?" I ask.

"It's not very big," you reply.

"Go get it, and I will get it in the mail for you right away," I assure you.

"It's not that easy," you say. "It has to be driven there. I'll give you $1,000."

Well, first, I don't have the time—the three or four days it would take to drive across the country. Remember, I live in Michigan. Second, my car isn't up for a trip like that—I'd need to get it checked out. Third, I have no vacation time left, and I would make more working at my job and certainly have less hassle. Come to think of it, I have three appointments I just cannot miss that week.

"Sorry," I say. "I would like to—but I just can't."

Now, let's dissect this for just a minute. I know you and like you. I know it would really help you out to do this tedious task for you. I also know I could do it if I really wanted to. The bottom line for me is, it's just not worth it.

But what if you said to me, "Dwight, if you drive the package across the country for me, I'll give you $100,000"? Or if you said the contents in this package would save my daughter's life, then what? I would instantly say, "Why haven't I left yet? Let's do it!"

You see, when the prize gets high enough, the "how" becomes easier. Suddenly, you figure out how to make it happen! Suddenly, you have the time! Suddenly, who cares about your clunker car— you'll rent, hitchhike, or even walk—whatever it takes!

So what motivated me? Was it the college education? Did it have to do with my culture or race? How about my religion? No— not even close. It went from my head to my heart. I knew all along that it would be nice to do it. But when it went from my head to my heart—in other words, when the prize was high enough—for whatever the reason—the how became easier.

Those who join America's Special Forces have to be cut of that cloth. Their focus must be absolute and single-minded.

And if this is true of America's Special Forces, who fight for their country, who fight for the safety of their families, who fight to preserve a free way of life—then imagine how true this must also be of God's Special Forces. Which, by the way, is the ultimate!

Why? Because while America's troops fight a war, God's Special Forces soldiers fight in the war behind all wars—the war that will soon end all wars.

I think I am starting to get excited. I want to be in God's Special Forces, don't you? But what is the cause? I know He came and died for my sins. That's what I have been told, anyway. I have read it in the Bible. I think that is absolutely wonderful, but it happened 2,000 years ago. That was a few years before I was born. Besides, I have been told it was all done at the cross. If that's the case, then why would God need any kind of special people?

It seems to me that just going to church, taking my Bible, and praising His name is good enough. Remember, there has to be a cause, you know—something that I not only believe in, but that I will get from my head to my heart. For me, as well as you, we have to get the prize high enough.

In order to get there, I can't wait till you read the next few chapters, where I share with you Top Secret information. We are going to go behind the scenes. We will go back thousands of years and look into the first war—a war that has been raging and devastating this earth and its inhabitants for 6,000 years. I believe that when you get through reading it, the prize will certainly be high enough. But I will let you make that call. Let's go!

THE BOTTOM LINE:

1. Being special is part of growth. Spiritually, what is the word used most often to describe growing in Jesus?

2. "When the price is high enough, the how becomes easier." What does this sentence mean to you?

3. What made Danny Dietz special? What drove him to make the sacrifice he did?

CHAPTER SIX

The Right Tools for the Job—Part I

My wife tells me that she's been hearing a rattling noise coming from under the hood of our car. So, fancying myself to be a fair mechanic, I go out to fix it. As I'm working away with the hood up, Deb comes out to see how I'm doing.

"What on earth?" she exclaims. "What have you done?"

I step back, proud of what I've accomplished.

"What do you mean?" I ask. And with my paintbrush in hand, I point to the newly painted engine. There it is—glistening in a fresh coat of blue latex enamel.

Now, you may think I'm just being facetious here, but I have a serious point to make. When you do a job, you simply *must* use the right tools! You don't fix engines with a paintbrush, any more than you paint your walls with a socket wrench.

In my military training—both in Army basic and later in Ranger Special Forces—it was vital that we learned how to use our equipment—the tools every soldier is issued. And when we enter God's Special Forces, we too need to learn how to use the tools God gives us for the mission He's called us to do for Him.

When I was in both basic and advanced military training, we were issued special equipment. Along with our physical and mental conditioning, an essential part of our training was to become proficient in using that equipment.

Of course, we were issued weapons—our rifles especially—and we had to learn how to care for them: how to clean them, to assemble and disassemble them, as well as to aim and fire them. We also had to know how to use other weapons: mortars, claymore mines, for example. But our primary weapon was the rifle, and we had to know it inside and out.

In addition to our rifle and other weapons, we had to become increasingly familiar with the *Ranger Manual*. In fact, we had to carry it everywhere we went in one of our pants' pockets—and if we were ever caught without it, we'd be ordered to drop and give the drill sergeant a vigorous batch of push-ups.

Now, as volunteers in God's Special Forces, what is the equipment every Christian must have? What are the primary tools we need to do the job God has for us?

THE MAIN WEAPON

For certain, just as my rifle was my main weapon—and just as my *Ranger Manual* was my guidebook, as a Christian, I have one great weapon—and one great manual. You see, the Bible—God's Word—is both.

"And take . . . the sword of the Spirit," Ephesians 6:17 says, "which is the word of God."

And Hebrews 4:12 adds this: "For the word of God is living and powerful, and sharper than any two-edged sword."

Before I volunteered for Army service, I worked—as mentioned in an earlier chapter—for my dad and uncle in construction. And I can tell you that if you don't know how to handle construction tools, you can really hurt somebody—either yourself or somebody else. People lose fingers—or worse—when they don't know how to handle circular or table saws, nail guns, and other tools. If you don't learn to handle it right, you can even mess up your thumb with a simple claw hammer.

When that happens, it's not the tool's fault. And it doesn't even mean that the person who mishandles the tool is a bad person. It does mean, though, it's just *so* important to develop skill in using the right tools.

The same is true of a military "tool"—a weapon. Whether we're talking the standard M16 rifle or one of its variants—or a sword, a weapon can do enormous damage if it's misused or mishandled by unskilled hands.

"Then Simon Peter, having a sword, drew it and struck the high priest's servant, and cut off his right ear. The servant's name was Malchus" (John 18:10).

Now, I haven't a clue why Peter, a fisherman and not a soldier, had a sword on him. But clearly, his lack of skill was dangerous. In fact, it's lucky for Malchus that Peter didn't hit where he likely was aiming—or that could have been the end of Malchus.

In and of itself, a weapon is neutral. It has no agenda. It's not angry at anyone. It's been designed for a purpose, however—to serve as a tool in the hands of a skilled soldier. And a weapon can be used both for offense and for defense in an attack. In the military, we had to learn how to use our weapons in both ways.

If a weapon has been designed to do damage—even to kill— why would God compare the Bible to a sword?

As we've noticed already in this book, there is a reason that even in the Bible itself, Christ compares His Church—His followers— to the military. In the previous chapter, we noted some of those verses. The inescapable fact is that this world is involved in the war of all wars—the great struggle between good and evil that began when Lucifer decided that He would submit to no one. He wanted to be His own god—to be totally in control of his own life without answering to his Creator.

This war that began in heaven has raged ever since; it is still going on. But it will not continue much longer. Christ said that

He would cut His work "short in righteousness" (Romans 9:28). God has had good reasons for letting the war continue this long. Sin has to be fully exposed for what it really is. As much as God hates it, only true love gives each of us free choices. Praise the Lord—we are living now near the final end of that war.

In a war, you *must* have weapons.

God has given us our M16: His Word. He has given us our two-edged Samurai sword: The Bible. And He needs us to become intimately familiar with it—to know it inside and out. Of course, just as in the U.S. Army, it takes time to become skilled in the use of weapons; it also takes time to become skilled in our knowledge of the Bible. In fact, it's a life-long process of growing ever more proficient.

If the Bible is our weapon, what do we do with it? How do we use God's Word as a weapon in this great war of all wars?

Some Christians have it all wrong. They're like Peter, swinging away wildly, trying to mow people down with their favorite Bible texts. Remember this: Peter cut off Malchus's ear. Jesus reattached it.

Think for a minute—what do you do with your ears? Listen, right? Of course! Many times, sadly enough, in my self righteousness I have taken out my razor-sharp, double-edged sword and not only whacked off one of my brother's or sister's ears, but like the most able Samurai, I've sliced off both ears before either of us knew what truly was happening.

Yet, Jesus Himself said, "Behold, I send you out. . . . Therefore be wise as serpents and harmless as doves" (Matthew 10:16). What? A sword....harmless? You see, we can't win people to Jesus by attacking them, by putting them down, by telling them they're wrong, by condemning them.

Then, what *does* it mean to use our sword or rifle as Christian soldiers? I can think of two things. First, we most certainly can use God's Word to condemn—not individual people—sin and evil in this world. As has often been said, "We are to hate the sin but love the sinner." Even when Jesus Himself rebuked the religious leaders of His time on earth, He was not attacking them personally. After all, He was their Creator. He was about to die to save them too.

But Jesus knew that if they were ever to repent and give up their rebellion against Him, they had to choose to separate themselves from their sins. So He used the sword of His own words in trying to separate themselves from their hypocrisy, their stubborn self-will, and their arrogant oppression of the people they led.

In returning to Hebrews 4:12, I want to add the rest of that verse:

> For the word of God is living and powerful, and sharper than any two-edged sword, piercing even to the division of soul and spirit, and of joints and marrow, and is a discerner of the thoughts and intents of the heart.

Did you see that? The sword pierces, it divides, and in the process, it reveals the "thoughts and intents of the heart." THIS is where God's Word as a sword is the most effective. And if we learn God's Word with the motive, not of attacking other people or showing them how wrong they are, but to show and speak it to them so the Holy Spirit can bring conviction to their hearts—then, my fellow volunteer in God's Special Forces—*then* we can "be all that we can be" for God!

CHANNELS TO REACH OTHERS

God has chosen to use people here on this earth to reach other people. Jesus cannot be personally here. He needs human hands to be His hands, human feet to go places for Him, human lips to speak His convicting truth. God is *depending* on us to be His channels to others here on earth.

I believe we take the statement "We just can't do anything—we are nothing," and one just as dangerous as that, "God doesn't need us," too far—in fact, way too far. God *does* need us. We are so precious to Him that He allowed His dear Son to die a death that only the worst criminals died. If He gave us free choice, then we certainly can do something—or we would be nothing but robots.

We are here for basically two reasons. One is to give our hearts to Him who died for us and then live by following His example. And two is, by that Christian example, to draw others to Jesus.

Many people say everything Jesus came to do was finished at the cross. Yet if that were true, why in the world are we still here? Christ did all He could at the cross. He paid the ultimate sacrifice. No one else could do what He did. He made a way for us to escape. He lived the life of the Lifegiver. His most precious gift to us was His own life!

He also gave us His example of self-sacrificing service by which to live. Because of His life and His words, He was crucified. We have to have both—Christ's life and His death—not just one. We have to have both—His example and His sacrifice. That's what gives Him the right to be our Captain in the Special Forces.

Satan's great argument in heaven was: "Why should we do what God says? We have our own minds. God created us perfect. We should be able to do what we want and still be in God's good graces." Remember that as a result war broke out, and Satan—along with one-third of the angels—was cast out. In looking at the three temptations of Jesus, every one of them had to do with obedience to God—even to the death of the cross.

Now, in these last days, we have a special work to do, and that work is second only in importance to Jesus dying on that cross. We are to show the world—as Christ did on this earth—that even though we are the weakest of the weak, in Christ we are strong. Think of it. After 6,000 years of degeneration our bodies are weaker. The planet is the far more polluted. We have nothing to brag about.

Yet, Christ says that our weaknesses will become our strengths through Him (2 Corinthians 12:9). When the end comes, from creation to probation, there will not be one human being who can say God was not fair—that Jesus had something we could not have. You see, there will be no excuse for not having victory in Jesus.

Do you see how important our special work is? I believe that angels would love to finish this work. If this work were only to tell people that Jesus died on the cross, Jesus could give everybody a dream when they went to sleep—a dream about the plan of salvation. But he hasn't done that. By way of His example set forth in His precious Word, He has given us the privilege of being His channels by living lives before others as to what He has done—and what He continues to do—for us. That is the everlasting gospel. Amazing grace!

So what happens if Jesus has daily opportunities for us—those "divine appointments" with others who need so desperately to hear and see His truth just for them—and we have nothing to say? We haven't learned the Word. We haven't become skilled in using it. That chance, at least, is lost. What we might have done never happens. The words we might have said remain unsaid. The shining example we could have been is just emptiness and darkness.

HARMONY THROUGH WORKING TOGETHER

But in sharing God's truth with others, we need to work together as followers of Jesus—not all by ourselves. Let me share what I mean. Four great singers all had equally beautiful voices. They were all brought together to sing a most glorious song. The director gave each of them the sheet music not only for the words but the music as well. All four of them loved the song. And all four of them thought that they should be the one to sing what they thought as the most important part.

When they got together the next day, they all furnished their own version of how it should be done. The director got them together and tapped his wand on his stand for them to start—and what happened next was almost unbearable. The sound that came to his experienced ears was like the sound of screeching tires and crashing metal. It was horrible. What had happened? How could the four best singers that he knew sound so bad?

The answer was simple. Instead of doing what they were supposed to do, they did what they thought was best. The result was nothing but utter failure. The good part of this story is that the director—although he wanted to—did not give up. He sat them down and said, "Do you see what happens to your beautiful voices when you each try to do it on your own? When you work together, one part will be as important and as melodious as the other. In fact, when you learn to share and blend in, the people watching and listening will not be able to tell who is singing which part."

Now let me say a few words about the other great item of military equipment we had to learn forward and backward in training: our *Ranger Manual.* How could we all work together in unison if we weren't all reading off the same page—or pages? How could we possibly know how to carry out our mission if we weren't clear on what it was? And how could we know what was required of us if we left our manuals closed and each of us just decided on our own what *we* thought was right—what *we* thought it meant to be a soldier?

What if we were happy to read the manual—but only parts of it? Parts of the *Ranger Manual* talk about killing your enemy. What if that is all you were to read? I know for a fact that you would become unbalanced. You would not know in every case how to deal with the enemy. You might say, "I read in my *Ranger's Manual* that I need to kill the enemy." As we all know, that is not always the case. Sometimes, the enemy might need to be interrogated for information. If only a part of that manual was read, then we might get it all wrong.

Who Needs a Manual?

It reminds me of a piece of equipment I bought not long ago. I remember being so excited when it finally arrived. I started to pull all the parts out of the boxes. My wife was looking on very curiously and asked, "Dwight, where is the manual?"

"Right here," I said. I grabbed it quickly and looked at it briefly— very briefly. I read a couple of captions on the pictures and said, "I understand it perfectly. Any dummy could put this together."

I handed the manual to my lovely wife and said, "I've got this thing down!"

Yea, right, Deb said, "Dwight, I know you did not read all the instructions. It says here to read them all before you begin. Don't you think the manufacturer knows a little more about this than you do? They designed it and built it."

While she was talking, I was quickly putting the pieces together.

"Look, Honey," I said. "I was not born yesterday. I have put many things together, and while you have been boring me with this nonsense about reading everything so I would not make a mistake, I have it half put together."

I was nearly finished putting it together, when, to my astonishment, I picked up a part that needed to be installed at the very beginning of this whole process. I tried everything under the sun to get this vitally important part installed—but without success. Needless to say, my wife sat there looking at me as if to say, "I told you so."

I had to take apart almost everything and start all over again. That one piece, as small as it was, made a huge difference. Now I look at the instructions or the manual in a new way. I know it is futile, and sometimes even dangerous, to read only parts of the manual or to put my own slant on it because it's what I think.

THE BIBLE: OUR WEAPON—OUR MANUAL

The Bible is not just our weapon in God's Army—it's also our manual. And like any manual, we need to use it wisely. We need to use it fairly. We need to consult it as our guide for the task we have been given.

We especially need to learn how to listen to exactly what the Bible is saying, instead of trying to find support in it for what we already believe or have heard.

For example, have you noticed how much confusion there is in the Christian world? The *World Christian Encyclopedia* identifies 10,000 distinct religions around the world. And just one of those religions—Christianity—is divided into 33,830 different denominations! And each of these denominations believes that it is the one true church of God on earth.

If entering the term *true church* into the largest Internet search engine—Google—substantially more than half a million entries are returned.

The Bible says there is "one Lord, one faith, one baptism; one God and Father of all" (Ephesians 4:5, 6). And for sure, we only have one Bible.

So how did this happen? How is it that 2,000 years after Jesus founded His "one church," it has split into more than 33,000 parts? How did such confusion happen?

Friends, it's true; we have only one Bible—one manual as volunteers in God's Army—but if we don't take time to know what it says, we're in trouble. And even if we do spend time learning it, we're in trouble if we misinterpret it or try to make it fit what *we* want it to say.

"Be diligent to present yourself approved to God," 2 Timothy 2:15 says, "a worker [we could also say *soldier*] who does not need to be ashamed, rightly dividing the word of truth."

What does it mean to "rightly divide" God's Word? How can we avoid ending up believing that the Bible says "B," when it really says "A"? Here's part of the answer:

"Knowing this first, that no prophecy of Scripture is of any private interpretation, for prophecy never came by the will of man, but holy men of God spoke as they were moved by the Holy Spirit" (2 Peter 1:20, 21).

Did you get that? *No private interpretation!* We can't bring to our study of the Bible our own preconceived ideas. We can't come to the Word to find ammunition to support our arguments. We can't decide what we think the Bible means, based on what we *want* it to mean—or even on what other people have *told* us it means. That is disastrous—and it's one of the chief reasons there is so much confusion in the Christian world. Even in my own church, I regret to say, there is far too much confusion on what the Bible teaches on this or that topic.

Did you also notice in that that text from 2 Peter that it said the

Bible writers did not write by "the will of man"—they didn't just write their own opinions and ideas? No, they wrote "as they were moved by the Holy Spirit." God the Holy Spirit is the true Author of the Bible.

So listen now: If we are to have any hope—any chance at all—of correctly understanding the Bible, we absolutely must surrender our own ideas, opinions, and interpretations, to the direct teaching of the Holy Spirit as we study the Word. That means we should never open its pages without praying not only that God will take away our self-will, but also that He will personally teach us what is truth.

"Lead me in Your truth and teach me," the psalmist wrote in Psalm 25:5. And John 16:13 says, "However, when He, the Spirit of truth, has come, He will guide you into all truth."

We've talked about rightly dividing the Word of truth. Because before we read our *Ranger Handbook*—the Bible—we need to come with a surrendered heart. But now, in addition to the weapon of the Word, I want to say more about another vital tool in our Special Forces service for God. I'm talking about the power of the Holy Spirit.

He will be the focus of our next chapter.

THE BOTTOM LINE:

1. A rifle is a soldier's main weapon. What is that weapon for a Christian? How exactly is this weapon to be used?

2. What happens when we ignore a manual? What happens when we ignore THE manual—the Bible?

3. How can it be that so many denominations believe so differently, when they each claim to base their beliefs on the same Bible?

CHAPTER SEVEN

The Right Tools for the Job—Part II

Who—or what—is the Holy Spirit?

Some are sure the Spirit is an unseen force or power that God issues. Such people believe that the Spirit is not a person but simply God's energy to get done what He wishes.

But I want to assure you that the Holy Spirit is not some energy wave or force. The Bible says that He is just as much God as are the Father and Jesus the Son. So understand that I would never suggest that we "use" God, as a soldier might use a rifle or even protective armor. We don't use God—God uses us!

But having said this, it's certainly right to say that the Holy Spirit provides power in our lives that we urgently need in order to accomplish the missions God sends us to do. So when I speak here of this vital "tool" available to us, I'm speaking of the Spirit's power. That is a tool God wants each of us to have—and if we ask for it, God will give it to us!

Jesus wants to send us the Holy Spirit. He said so before He left our earth to return to heaven. After Jesus had departed, the Holy

Spirit's power came over Peter and the other apostles. And here's part of what Peter then said:

"Then Peter said unto them, Repent, and be baptized every one of you in the name of Jesus Christ for the remission of sins, and ye shall receive the gift of the Holy Ghost" (Acts 2:38).

Do you see the prerequisite for receiving the Holy Spirit? *Repent.* In other words, "turn around" (the Bible's original Greek language here means "to think differently," to "turn around"). Then, Peter said, be baptized. By the way, Peter says it in just that order: repent—turn around—and *then* be baptized, which means to die to self. And dying to self means, "Not my will, Lord, but Yours." Then Jesus truly can be the Lord of your life—not your Saviour only. The truth is, when Jesus comes into our lives, He won't and can't come as just our Saviour, without also being our Lord!

As we read the precious Word of God, we have the great opportunity of hearing the Holy Spirit's voice. It's important to listen to that voice. Just remember that we need to qualify that voice—be sure it is in fact the Holy Spirit speaking by the Word of God. The power of the Holy Spirit is a vital tool—an indispensable part of our equipment as God's Special Forces. But used wrongly, or mistaken for some "counterfeit" tool, it can bring utter destruction.

"Feels Good" Religion

This mightily important tool does not come easy at all. I know from painful experience. It is sad to see that many times we cheapen the work of the Holy Spirit. We want Him to make us feel emotionally happy. We want to jump up and down in church. I have seen people almost in a trance or frenzy—I call this the "feels good" religion—only for them to go back home and yell at their children or spouses. Are you getting the picture? Have any of you ever cheated on your taxes, or maybe you bought something at a store and when you went to pay for it, the checkout person made a mistake and gave you too much money back? The Holy Spirit is working on our hearts, saying, "You know this is not right. What would Jesus do?" In the quietness of our minds—because of the greatest gift that Jesus could ever give us, the Holy Spirit who convicts us—we know it is not the Christian thing to do.

The Spirit convicts us of sin. Let's read what Paul has to say in Acts 24:24 and 25: "And after certain days, when Felix came with his wife Drusilla, which was a Jewess, he sent for Paul, and heard him concerning the faith in Christ. And as he reasoned of righteousness, temperance, and judgment to come, Felix trembled, and answered, Go thy way for this time; when I have a convenient season, I will call for thee."

See, part of the Holy Spirit's job is to convict us of sin. That is why His power and presence in our lives is such a great gift. The problem is that it takes time to hear and know the Holy Spirit's voice. I have had so many people come to me after I have spoken of this great gift and ask, "How do you hear the Holy Spirit? I have tried to—but I've been unsuccessful."

I certainly can relate to that. One key is that before we can have the tool of the Holy Spirit's power to use in our service for God, that tool must first be applied to our own lives. When that happens, it's like the power of the Holy Spirit focusing in on our own life. It's like a honing or chiseling tool. It can hurt, big time. It can be like an elephant stepping on your toes. But when it's through hurting—wow! What a peace and delight we can experience!

Jesus says that we are the branches, and He is the vine. In order to produce big, tasty fruit, we need to be pruned. What a trying process! But again, the end result is heavenly.

Another key to hearing the Spirit's voice is to listen carefully. The Holy Spirit speaks in a still, small voice. He speaks in the recesses of your conscience. I have often prayed to God and said, "Lord, speak to me, but louder please—because I can't hear You."

We need to be quiet. But to learn to listen takes time. Elijah needed to learn to listen—and not just when he wanted to listen. The story is found in 1 Kings 19:9-18. The Holy Spirit did not speak in the wind, earthquake, or fire, but in the still, small voice. Also, take a look at Isaiah 30:15, and then Isaiah 30:21.

Let me share an example from my own life. Before I begin, I want you to know that this happened after much training on my part in learning to listen.

ARGUING WITH THE HOLY SPIRIT

It was a beautiful sunny morning, and Deb and I decided to take a walk. Now, even though it was beautiful outside, it was also about 20 below zero. I mean, teeth-chattering cold! But there was no wind, and the sun was brilliantly putting forth its shining rays, making the white wonderland outside sparkle like a treasure chest of precious gems. We could hardly wait to bundle up and get outdoors.

Once in the outdoors, we started talking about anything and everything. We were just enjoying each other's company.

Then it happened—with no warning whatever.

Deb said something, and I couldn't believe she said it. I can't remember now just what she said, but I know that back then, I felt it was absolutely uncalled for. So I said the same thing back, to let her know that I would give her a little taste of her own medicine.

You'll never guess what happened next. She said something even worse! Can you believe that? I don't remember what that was, either. Not to be outdone, I came back with something strong enough that she pulled her hand out of mine and started walking slower than me.

The real battle had began. I had learned to tune in to the Holy Spirit, but I still had not learned yet to keep Him tuned in all the time. As I walked ahead of my precious princess, feeling more than a little bit hurt, that still, small voice said, with no warning, "Dwight, turn around, and say you're sorry to Deb."

"No," I said in my heart—my conscience—"she started it."

"Does it matter, Dwight? Did I not call you to be the husband—the house band—the priest, the leader, the protector?"

"Yes, Lord, and that's exactly why she should say she is sorry first. Since I am the leader and all that other stuff, she will think I am a wimp if I just give in. Lord, it's just not fair."

So I kept walking. But then the Lord spoke to my heart and said, "Dwight, did you do everything right? Was your response in me—or in the carnal flesh?"

"Ouch! Lord, You certainly know how to hit a guy where it hurts."

"Dwight, will you surrender your carnal heart to me right now?"

"But what about Deb? Are You speaking to her?"

"What does it matter to you? Does that change things with us?"

"Well, no, Lord—I guess not."

Have you ever tried arguing with the Lord through His Holy Spirit? I have yet to win the argument. So, in the quietness of my mind, with no other distractions, I yielded my selfish flesh in exchange for God's great gift. Was it painful? Oh, yes! Was it worth it? You be the judge.

I turned around, and Deb was probably a hundred feet behind me by now. She had her head down and was kicking the snow as she was walking.

"Deb," I said. She raised her head and gave me that look that only we husbands would know.

"I am so sorry, Deb. Will you forgive me?"

I saw tears immediately pop out of her eyes like rockets. Her first and precious words were, "Yes," and then between tears, "I am sorry too—will you forgive me?"

We knelt together right there and asked the God of heaven and earth to continue to give us this great gift. What an amazing, awesome tool is the power of the Holy Spirit in our lives—as well as in our service.

Another mighty work of the Holy Spirit is to bring unity among Christ's followers. Just before His disciple Judas betrayed Him, Jesus prayed for not only His disciples but for all His followers who would come later—including you and me. In his prayer, He said, "Father, keep through Your name those whom You have given Me, that they may be one as We are" (John 17:11).

To me, 33,830 denominations doesn't sound like "one." And in any one of those churches, the division will be even greater. This is the sad result of each man and woman following Adam and Eve in deciding that *they* know best—that they are wise enough to interpret and correctly understand God's Word.

If we really do surrender to the Holy Spirit to be taught, He will most certainly help us do what we need to do in order to avoid reaching totally wrong conclusions as we read the Bible. One of those things He will help us consistently do is remember what Isaiah 28:10 says: "For precept must be upon precept, precept upon precept, line upon line, line upon line, here a little, there a little."

Do you know what this is saying? It's talking about comparing Scripture with Scripture—comparing one verse with others. It is so dangerous to take just one Bible verse—or even a couple of them—and reach a conclusion based on such a limited part of the Word.

Many churches have doctrines that are built entirely on just one verse—a verse that ignores the context—the verses right around it, to say nothing of all the other verses in God's Word that speak on that topic. If we are dishonest and careless in reading the Bible, we can make it support practically anything!

An extreme example some provide is how the Bible teaches the "doctrine of suicide." Say what? Well, of course! Does the Bible not say that "Judas went out and hanged himself"? And does it not also say in another place "Go, and do thou likewise"? Can you see how foolish such a conclusion would be? Yet, many churches have entire basic doctrines that are built on just such a shaky and dishonest use of God's Word.

As committed soldiers in God's Army, we don't take our orders from anyone but God Himself. Even in our own church, and with our own teachers and preachers, we need to follow the example of the Bereans mentioned in Acts 17:11, who "received the word with all readiness of mind, and searched the scriptures daily, whether those things were so."

Yes, these Bereans listened to the apostles preaching and teaching, but they didn't just take the words of any man, even an apostle. They "searched the scriptures daily" for themselves, to see "whether those things were so."

It's Not About Being Right

Fellow soldiers, we need to be diligent and serious and careful about how we study our manual—the Bible. We need to "rightly divide" it. We need to set aside and surrender our own opinions as we study it, letting its Author, the Holy Spirit, teach us. We need to compare each text with everything else the Bible says on that topic. Then—and this is very hard for that carnal flesh to do—we need not worry about protecting ourselves. It's not about you and I being right but about God being vindicated because *He* is right. He is perfect. It doesn't matter if we have believed what we thought was truth since our birth. It doesn't even matter if Mom and Dad or Grandpa and Grandma believed the same thing. The question should never be: "What will people say? Or, "How will that look? But "What is the truth?" When the Holy Spirit convicts us, it is time to follow that even though we might become castaways. Remember, Grandma and Grandpa could have believed the wrong thing and still be saved because the Holy Spirit never convicted them on that subject.

If we truly search for truth, we'll know our manual well. We'll be ready then to be of great use to God, as He calls us to meet His daily "divine appointments."

And when we learn to use our Christian military equipment rightly—we'll also know how to use the Word as our weapon against sin and the wily enemy who is seeking to destroy not just us, but everyone around us.

God has given us the right tools for the job.

Let's become experts in using them, what do you say?

THE BOTTOM LINE:

1. In chapter 6, one of the tools available to a Christian soldier is identified as God's Word. What is the one identified in this chapter?

2. Do any of us ever try to do the Holy Spirit's work of producing conviction of sin in others? If that work is His, what is ours, in winning others to Jesus?

3. Which is more important: talking to the Spirit, or listening to Him?

CHAPTER EIGHT

Fit to Fight

An old-time farmer can tell you that sitting on a solid, sturdy three-legged stool to milk Bossy works just fine. But if one or more of those legs is missing, the stool is suddenly unstable. I'm fascinated by how often in the Bible, the number "three" comes up:

▶ The Father, Son (Jesus), and Holy Spirit.

▶ The way God created us, we have a threefold nature: mental, physical, and spiritual.

▶ In John 14:6, Jesus said: "I am the way, the truth, and the life."

▶ Jesus picked three disciples to be more closely associated with Him than the other nine.

Looking at that third one, we might say too that there are three parts to our training as volunteers in God's Special Forces:

1. **The Way:** Jesus lived as our example to show us this way— to show us what to do, how to act. Our "doing," we could call the "physical" part of our mission.

2. **The Truth:** God reveals His truth to us in the Bible, showing us what we should think. We could call this the "mental" part of our mission.

3. **The Life:** The Holy Spirit convicts us and lives Christ's life through us. So this could be the "spiritual" part of our mission.

As we consider this threefold mission, I'd like to ask a favor. Please indulge me in a short word study. I'd like to take a close-up look for a moment at the term *Special Forces.* I'll start with the second word first. (Since I'm writing this book, I can do things like that!)

Now, the word *forces* is familiar to nearly everybody. If you want, you can look it up in your favorite dictionary, but basically what you'll find is that *forces* means "a group of people who are able to work together to get something done."

When applied to the military, the word means something like "a unit trained to obey orders and work together to oppose an enemy."

If the word *force* is traced back to see where it came from, its roots are found in an old Latin word—*fortis,* meaning "strong." So *forces*—the plural—is about people working together toward a goal. The idea has to do with "strength in numbers."

Enough on the second word. How about *special?* Again, in going back to find the root of *special,* the definition reads something like this: "marked off from others by some distinguishing quality."

So let's try to put special forces together: "A group of people different from others, who become strong by working together to achieve something."

The United States military has its branches of the armed forces: Army, Navy, Air Force, Marines, and National Guard. The men and women in the armed forces are committed to working together to get something done—to oppose any enemy and protect the homeland.

But within the branches of the armed forces are the elite

Special Forces—those who are truly "marked off from others by some distinguishing quality." Or, in this case, by *a number* of distinguishing qualities.

Special Forces are special! They . . .

- ▶ Have special advanced combat training
- ▶ Take on special assignments
- ▶ Wear special uniforms
- ▶ Operate special equipment and weapons
- ▶ Have distinguishing marks: badges and other insignia
- ▶ Have a special dietary regimen
- ▶ Undergo rigorous fitness training

In this chapter, I want to look with you at those last two areas—special diet and special fitness training. You see, when you're training to go into battle, you absolutely must be in peak physical condition. If the word *force* means "strong," then that's exactly what you need to be!

The demands of battlefield combat are strenuous. And if you aren't at your physical best, you're likely to be defeated. It can mean the difference between life and death. If this is true of regular combat troops, imagine how important diet and fitness are to the elite Special Forces.

When I moved beyond basic training in the Army into training for the Airborne Rangers, we had our own area for eating our meals—and our own customized diet designed to give us the maximum in strength and endurance. And of course, everybody knows that as tough as regular Army training is, Special Forces training is even more demanding.

When I first went into the recruiting office, I was basically just killing some time—just idly curious. But then I heard things that made me perk right up. I heard that in the military—especially in the Rangers—I'd be *special*. I can't begin to tell you what a driving force that was for me! I'd wanted all my life to be somebody special!

I also heard them say that they'd make me "lean and mean." I was already lean—maybe a little too lean. I wanted to be, as they'd say today, really ripped! I wanted muscles that could be noticed. I wanted to see if I could work without a shirt and have six-pack abs and rock-hard biceps to show for it.

Anyone who knows anything about military training, knows that I more than got my wish. If Army basic training didn't get me all the way there, Ranger training certainly did. I came out of that time of my life in the best shape ever.

All through this book, we've been comparing military Special Forces with God's Special Forces. And I want to tell you that the high-intensity training and specialized diet that made us into a precision, fearsome fighting force for Uncle Sam is just as indispensable when we volunteer for God's Special Forces.

The original terrorist is on the loose and hates not only God—he hates that you and I even exist. He wants to take us down. We're down to the final battle in the greatest war ever fought, and Satan is pulling out all the stops to take out as many men, women, and children as he can.

He is attacking on all fronts:

- ▶ He's amping up his hate-propaganda campaign against God.

- ▶ He's deceiving as many Christians as he can, misleading them into false teachings.

- ▶ With the end coming fast, he's trying to divert everyone's attention, keeping them amused and entertained and stressed and busy.

- ▶ He's especially opposing God's last-day Special Forces: those who volunteer to be part of the elite for God, and those who are willing to do whatever it takes to carry out God's final mission here on Earth.

Here's the Bible's warning: "Be sober, be vigilant; because your adversary the devil walks about like a roaring lion, seeking whom he may devour." 1 Peter 5:8.

We are going to need every bit of health and fitness and

conditioning we can get, as we try to do God's work here in this world. For the kind of mission for which God needs us, we need to be able to have amazing mental and physical fitness. We need to have energy to burn. And we need to be able to think quickly and clearly.

I need to say those two things again: *We need to have energy to burn. And we need to be able to think quickly and clearly.*

THE MIND-BODY LINK

Science and medicine have increasingly discovered in recent years that there is a close, inseparable link between the mind and the body. Whatever affects one affects the other. So we can't focus on just being physically fit for God's service. We also have to concentrate on our mental and spiritual conditioning as well.

One thing this means is that if my body isn't what it should be, my mind isn't going to be clear. Even my ability to communicate with God spiritually is going to suffer. So remember that while one great reason to concentrate on being physically fit for God's service is because we'll have more energy and less disease, a healthy body also means a healthy mind and spirit.

Does God have anything to say to us about diet and fitness for His Special Forces volunteers? Absolutely! In great detail, He shares in our great training manual—the Bible—just what we need to get into, and stay in, peak condition.

The military likes to say that they take "raw" untrained, unfit recruits and make soldiers out of them. Well, God goes one better. He made each of us in the first place—and then if we volunteer, He "remakes" us so that we're the best we can be! This reminds me of the U.S. Army slogan: "Be all that you can be." God wants to make me—and He wants to make you—all that we can be. All that He *knows* we can be!

But for that to happen, we can't just sit down next to the manual (the Bible) and hope that what it says about how to eat and how to be healthy will just sort of magically seep into us and transform us into highly conditioned men and women. Now, as a big sports shoe company says, we also have to "just do it." And God is available to help us as we choose to get ourselves into shape.

I don't know whether at this moment, you're healthy or unhealthy. I don't care if you're built like an athlete or more like a great big marshmallow. I don't care if you run marathons or get winded walking up a flight of stairs. That really isn't what's important. What IS important is that wherever you are physically, you join me in following the best possible diet and fitness program you possibly can. If you're out of shape, that will get you into shape. If you're already in shape, it will keep you there.

God's Special Forces Diet

All through history, God has given a special diet to those He calls to carry out special missions for Him.

God gave Samson a special diet. John the Baptist had a special diet. For forty years, the children of Israel also had a special diet—manna—to help prepare them for when they would enter the Promised Land of Canaan.

And in the New Testament, Paul wrote this in Romans 12:1: "I beseech you therefore, brethren, by the mercies of God, that you present your bodies a living sacrifice, holy, acceptable to God, which is your reasonable service."

We too are preparing to enter a new and even better Promised Land than Israel did—Canaan, the Promised Land of heaven. So it's important that our diet be a part of our preparation.

Perhaps one of the most striking examples of the powerful link between diet and our spiritual service is found in the Old Testament story of Daniel and his friends. So look with me for a minute at the book of Daniel. It may already be a familiar story, how Daniel and some of his young Israelite friends were captured when King Nebuchadnezzar of Babylon invaded Jerusalem. The king took the young men back to train them for his royal service.

The training period was to last three years, and during that time, the trainees were to eat the king's prescribed diet. Even though he was young, Daniel and some of his friends knew a better way—a diet their God had shown them.

> But Daniel purposed in his heart that he would not defile himself with the portion of the king's meat, nor with the wine which he drank: therefore he requested of the prince of the eunuchs that he might not defile himself (Daniel 1:8, KJV).

Daniel's request put fear into the king's servant—a man named Melzar. If he let Daniel and his friends do this, and they ended up weak and sickly, he could lose more than his job—he'd likely lose his head! But Daniel proposed a test.

> Prove thy servants, I beseech thee, ten days; and let them give us pulse to eat, and water to drink. Then let our countenances be looked upon before thee, and the countenance of the children that eat of the portion of the king's meat: and as thou seest, deal with thy servants.

> So he consented to them in this matter, and proved them ten days. And at the end of ten days their countenances appeared fairer and fatter in flesh than all the children which did eat the portion of the king's meat.

> Thus Melzar took away the portion of their meat, and the wine that they should drink; and gave them pulse (Daniel 1:12-16).

Amazing! After only ten days—ten days!—Daniel and his friends looked far healthier than all the other trainees. And all because of a specialized diet that God had already shown the children of Israel centuries earlier!

Pulse—and water.

Water, we know about. So what is *pulse?* Basically, pulse is a word that describes a vegetarian diet. The king's diet was rich in meat and wine. But God knew that He had designed men and women originally to be at their best with a vegetarian diet.

According to the Bible, only after the Flood did God approve some flesh foods to become a part of human diet. But even then, He made clear that some meat is "clean," while some is "unclean." He explains all this in Leviticus chapter 11, and Deuteronomy chapter 14. I won't take time to list all the clean animals and the unclean ones—although I'd recommend that those chapters be read.

Suffice it to say, though, that among the "unclean" meats God mentioned as unfit for food are swine products (that would include pork, bacon, and ham), shellfish and many other seafood items, and creatures that are basically scavengers.

If you pay much attention at all to the news, you hear more and more about the downside of a meat diet: diseases, cholesterol, antibiotics, hormones, high fat and urea content, and chemical additives, among others.

In addition, meat takes far longer to digest, so the "transit time" of food through the system is slowed dramatically. This means that meat that's consumed, sits for long periods in the colon, creating putrefactive bacteria and toxins. It's little wonder that a meat diet is linked with higher risk of colon and other cancers, as well as liver disease, kidney failure, and gallstones.

All kinds of scientific and statistical information could be assembled showing the risks of a meat diet. Let me just offer this one example of scores that might be mentioned: Did you know that a one-pound, well-done steak contains four to five micrograms of benzopyrene—a major cancer-causing substance? The benzopyrene in just that one steak is equivalent to what a person would get from smoking 300 cigarettes!

All these scientific facts and statistics aside, though, you know too of the risks increasingly reported in the media about a meat diet: Mad Cow Disease, frequent recalls of E. coli—tainted meat, and appalling filthy conditions in meat-packing plants.

Maybe you could choose to avoid the "unclean" meats the Bible lists in Leviticus 11. Maybe you could choose to be extra-careful and eat only the better meats from the supermarket.

But good is *always* the enemy of the best! God wants the absolute best for us. And God originally gave us the best diet possible, so we could be at our personal best physically, mentally, and spiritually.

If we go back to the beginning—to what God gave human beings to eat, as recorded in the book of Genesis—we find that this diet consisted of fruits, vegetables, and grains, with some use too of nuts, seeds, and herbs.

A vegetarian diet not only avoids completely the dangers of a meat diet, but it has many positive benefits too. It's low in fat. It's high in fiber. It's filled with nutrients, which are largely stripped out of processed foods.

On a vegetarian diet, it's far easier to achieve and maintain an ideal body weight. It is also highly protective against the leading lifestyle diseases that cause the most deaths: heart disease, cancer, stroke, respiratory diseases, and diabetes—currently in that order.

Speaking of these diseases, there's another deadly enemy of good health, so clearly proven now as a cause of disease and death that no one can dispute it—and that is tobacco. Tobacco in any form will do great damage to human health. The same is true for alcohol, for caffeinated beverages, and for drugs—especially illegal drugs, but also many prescribed ones that are misused.

WRITE IT ON A CARD AND TAPE IT WHERE YOU CAN SEE IT!

Remember what Daniel and his friends did for ten days? They ate *pulse* (a vegetarian diet)—and water. Let's not forget the water! Most people simply do not drink enough water to be at their optimum level of good health. They only drink when they feel "thirsty." Thirst, though, is not a dependable guide. If we only drink when we feel thirsty, we're more than likely going around dehydrated most of the time.

Most of us have heard this advice our whole lives. We should drink six to eight glasses of water a day—minimum. When we're doing physical work, or "working out," or when the weather is hot, we will need far more.

So write on a card somewhere—"More Water!"—and tape it up someplace where you're likely to see it often. Learn all you can about the quality of your water. Find out if your public water supply is a good source. Some public water is excellent—some is terrible in terms of the toxins and bacteria it may contain. Bottled water, besides being expensive, has been shown in many cases to be no better than tap water. In fact, the leading brands *are* tap water that's just been processed. On the other hand, some bottled water—just as some tap water—is excellent.

Once you've settled on what your source of water will be, drink up! Your billions of body cells will thank you for it! You'll flush your whole system and keep it in good running order.

If Diet Is One Oar, the Other Is...

We've talked now at some length about diet. It's time to say a few things about fitness. Yes, we're bringing in that word that so many don't want to hear: exercise. Just as God made us to run on the highest quality fuel (food), He also designed us to *move*.

I don't need to present an in-depth review of all the benefits of exercise. We already know the most important ones: strength, endurance, weight management, energy, better sleep, better functioning at every level. And the benefits of exercise aren't all physical. Exercise gets oxygen to the brain so we think more clearly. It lifts our mood by raising levels of certain brain chemicals: endorphins, dopamine, serotonin, and others.

When we exercise, we'll have better memory, think more quickly and be less likely to develop mental degeneration.

Both diet and exercise are essential to fend off disease, to help us feel and look our best, and to help us be "peak performers."

Fellow volunteer, in God's Special Forces, the special diet and fitness training God gives us to be part of His elite is *not optional!* If we are serious about being in His Special Forces—if we really want to have the physical stamina to carry out God's critical missions here in the final days of earth, we must submit to His rigorous training.

Some Christians almost scoff at other Christians who seem to emphasize health and diet a lot. They think it's a sign of being "rigid," or "legalistic," or at the very least, "uptight." But if we are truly going to be spiritual antiterrorists, if we really are going to battle against a "roaring lion," we'd better be ready for it, what do you say?

Satan loves it when he can lure Christians into the ditch on either side of the road to Heaven. On one side is a ditch where diet and health can indeed become a matter of rules and legalism—of living a certain way in order to win or stay in God's good graces. This ditch is filled with the terrible sewage of trying to be saved by our good works instead of what Jesus has done.

The other side of the road has a ditch that's just as deadly. That's the one where the devil has one of his counterfeits for real faith. Those in this ditch, he has brainwashed to say, "Since we're not saved by how we live, it doesn't even matter what you eat or do, whether you exercise or not, how physically fit you are or not. All we have to do is say we love Jesus."

We must avoid these ditches—these counterfeits and extremes —and stay on the road that leads to heaven. That road avoids both legalism and license. It avoids both salvation BY works and salvation WITHOUT works. Instead, it cultivates a faith THAT works by love.

There is so much more that I could say about diet and fitness— about the specifics of great health that this chapter just introduces. There are many books and articles to be found on the Internet. Just remember Satan always has his counterfeits. Check it out thoroughly.

Special Forces. Those words still make my pulse run faster. I love being part of something really big—something that challenges me to my limits—something that I can do in this life that will make a huge difference.

There IS no greater challenge to which we can rise than to enlist in God's service. Long ago at the lonely cross of Calvary, God gave His Son—His absolute best—for us. I want to give back to Him *my* absolute best, so that other souls may have the choice for eternal life. Don't you?

THE BOTTOM LINE:

1. The Rangers take pride in being "lean and mean." Should Christians also sense the importance of being physically fit? Why IS this important for someone who aspires to be in God's Special Forces?

2. In this chapter, two "oars in the water" of fitness were explored. What were they?

3. Toward what two extremes about physical fitness does Satan work to lure us?

CHAPTER NINE

God's Military Dress Code

Doctor, lawyer, merchant, chief...

Or so the old saying goes. Now, let's say we saw these four standing side by side. Think we could tell them apart?

Of course we could! And how? Well, the doctor would likely be wearing a long white coat and a stethoscope around his neck. The lawyer—perhaps a business suit, silk tie, and an expensive watch. The merchant? Let's say a full-length apron emblazoned with the name of his store. And the chief—let's say an American Indian chief—would wear leather, beads, and a feather head-dress.

We can tell a lot about people by what they wear.

How people dress may indeed be related to their work. But it also can be connected to some organization to which they belong. For example:

▶ Boy Scouts and Girl Scouts
▶ Nurses
▶ Players on the New York Yankees baseball team
▶ Housekeeping staff in an upscale hotel
▶ Students in a Catholic parochial school

- ▶ Employees of Federal Express or UPS
- ▶ Airline pilots and flight attendants
- ▶ Even prisoners in a penitentiary!

In addition to these examples, perhaps no people are more readily identifiable by their uniforms than members of the armed forces. Military uniforms vary from one branch of the service to another and from one country to another. But a military uniform is among the most recognizable forms of clothing on earth.

When I joined the military, along with all other recruits, I was issued the standard clothing of a soldier in Uncle Sam's Army. Later, when I moved on to advanced Special Forces training as an Army Airborne Ranger, I was issued new and distinctive clothing unique to the elite Rangers.

Some of our Ranger clothing was designed for use in training and combat conditions. But we also were issued formal, full-dress uniforms for public occasions. And I can tell you that we were proud of those uniforms! And with good reason.

OUR UNIFORMS SET US APART—SAID TO OTHERS THAT WE WERE SPECIAL

A soldier walks through an airport or enters a store, and instantly people see that he or she belongs to a special organization with a special mission. Yes, those uniforms make their wearers stand out. But do you think they are embarrassed or self-conscious to be seen in those uniforms?

Absolutely not! Those of us who wear or have worn our military uniforms were proud. We felt honored, chosen, and special.

And if wearing the uniform of a branch of the armed services made us feel that way, imagine how it felt to wear the uniform of an elite member of the Special Forces!

OUR UNIFORMS SYMBOLIZED OUR UNITY—OUR SOLIDARITY

Yes, it was a good feeling to realize that civilians noticed our uniforms and realized our special role in protecting and defending their freedoms. But our uniforms also built unity between those of us who wore them. We were in this together. We were all for one—and one for all.

OUR UNIFORMS WERE A SYMBOL OF HOW INTERDEPENDENT AND MUTUALLY SUPPORTIVE WE WERE

We were each needed and important members of a team effort. What we wore helped build morale and "esprit de corps."

In battle conditions, uniforms become even more important, marking, as they do, the difference between friendly forces and the enemy.

OUR UNIFORMS WERE DESIGNED FOR A PURPOSE

No one will ever accuse soldiers of making a "fashion statement"! You never see servicemen parading the latest military clothing on a catwalk or modeling for the catalogs of exclusive stores.

OUR UNIFORMS WERE DESIGNED TO FIT OUR MISSION

Made of durable fabric, our uniforms provided a layer of protection for crawling through dirt and sand and fending off insects and the sun's burning rays.

But our uniforms also provided camouflage. In battle, the last thing we needed was to call attention to ourselves! We certainly did not want to reveal our position to the enemy by letting the sun's rays flash from the surface of shiny metal items. The plainer we dressed, the better.

Even our formal dress uniforms sent their own message. Clean. Well-pressed. Shoes and buckles shined to a mirror finish. Caps perfectly positioned. Everything about those dress uniforms telegraphed quality, attention to detail, and the pride of being among the elite fighting forces of our nation.

OUR UNIFORMS SENT A MESSAGE ABOUT OUR NATION

What difference, it might be asked, could it possibly make how a single soldier dresses? If America is the "land of the free," shouldn't that freedom extend to its military, so that each soldier gets to choose what he or she wears?

Let's run with that idea, then.

You see TV coverage of a Special Forces platoon as they prepare for deployment on a vital, classified mission on the other side of the globe. The commander has on Bermuda shorts and a tank top emblazoned with the name and faces of his favorite rock group. His female assistant is dressed in the provocative clothing you would expect to find a streetwalker wearing.

Various other platoon members have on low-slung baggy pants that scuff the ground as they walk, dirty blue jeans with frayed holes all over them, or cowboy boots and large belt buckles.

What would be your overall impression of the country this ragtag bunch represents? Would it inspire confidence? Would it say anything to you about how serious these Special Forces troops were about their mission? Would it tell you anything about their level of discipline and commitment? And above all, what would all this say about the nation these service men and women represent?

Ultimately, what would the attire of these Special Forces soldiers say about their commander in chief?

Now, after reading this, what does all this discussion of military uniforms have to do with us today? Maybe a lot more than many might think!

When I was in the American Special Forces, how we dressed—as you can see—was important in many ways. We didn't go to boot camp and expect we could take our clothes from home and dress any way we chose.

Guys who showed up—whether in blue jeans and T-shirts or vested suits—had to surrender those and wear military-issue duds instead. Anybody who showed up with gold chains, earrings, or other forms of jewelry also had to remove those. As I mentioned earlier, we even had to give up our carefully coiffed hair and spend our service time for Uncle Sam wearing a buzz cut.

Now here's my point—the main point of this chapter: If it was important how we dressed to be in America's Special Forces, it is even more important how we dress as members of God's Special Forces!

And as it happens, in His manual (the Bible), God has set forth very plainly how His last-day Special Forces are to dress.

IS DRESSING GOD'S WAY LEGALISM?

But oh, someone protests. This is legalism! We have to give up our freedom to dress as we wish because if we don't, God won't save us.

Say *what?*

Nowhere in His Word does God even once say anything of the sort! Our means of salvation was accomplished at the cross of Calvary. We are asked to dress a certain way, not so we can be saved, but because we ARE saved! We also dress a certain way because—like American Special Forces, our dress helps us carry out our special mission!

As our commander in chief in the war of all wars, God knows that in the final battle, even our clothing matters. With God, everything is important—even small details make a difference. Shouldn't we be free just to dress as we please? You know, those who are truly committed to their mission—whether in the military or in God's Army—just don't ask, "What's the least I can get away with?" They know they are foot soldiers and are not in charge—someone higher up is. For Christian soldiers, the question is: "Will Christ be the Lord and Master of my life—or will I?"

When we choose Jesus as our Lord, we trust His wisdom. We know He has good reasons for what He asks of us. We know that when we let Him be in charge, our lives will be far more peaceful and effective.

As an example of what I'm writing here, if the Lord were to ask me to crawl on my hands and knees—starting tomorrow—for the rest of my life, I would want to ask Him, "Lord, do I have to wait until tomorrow? Can I start now?"

I would hope that were God to ask me something like that, I'd trust Him as my Savior and Lord, knowing that He will only ask me to do what's best for my life—and for my ability to influence others for Him. I certainly hope I'd never respond: "Lord, not *that*—at least give me another year or two."

So just what *does* God ask of us in this area of dress? It's really not all that complicated. Let's review the few principles of dress God has set out for us:

1. THE PRINCIPLE OF MODESTY

Paul wrote: "...in like manner also, that the women adorn themselves in modest apparel, with propriety and moderation" (1 Timothy 2:9).

Some of you may have lived long enough to remember a time when modesty in dress was common not only among church members but in the general public as well. Times have certainly changed.

Seemingly all barriers of real modesty have fallen. In the media, anything goes, and everything shows.

Modesty is so uncommon that perhaps a quick review of what it even is could be useful. One dictionary meaning is a "reserve in appearance, speech, and behavior"—in other words, holding something back, especially when it comes to sexual matters. The word *modesty* also includes "a reticence to draw attention to oneself, simplicity, and moderation."

Why is modesty still important—especially important—for God's last-day followers, His Special Forces? Because God knows that the mission to which He calls us is so vital, so absolutely critical and urgent, that any distraction could be deadly. If people can't hear us for focusing on how we look, they may miss a life-and-death warning or opportunity God is trying to get through to them.

God also knows—as so eloquently explained in the New Testament—that the flesh and the spirit are at war. If we feed one, the other starves. If we Christians wear immodest clothing, it only encourages the fleshly or carnal—and our spiritual growth is threatened.

Sexual immodesty is especially damaging too, in that it threatens marriages and families.

Can we really afford to risk all this by indulging in wearing anything that violates this Bible principle of modesty?

2. THE PRINCIPLE OF INNER VERSUS OUTER ADORNMENT

God sees the past, present, and future. He knew that in the end times, people would be faced with all kinds of problems and temptations. He knew that people would struggle with diet—with fast-food joints on seemingly every street corner. He knew that poor diet choices would lead to all kinds of terrible, life-threatening health problems.

He also knew that in the last days, people would be caught up in how they look. Fashion would be an enormous influence. And He knew that people would spend far too much time and money trying to decorate themselves—or even worse, mutilate themselves with piercings and tattoos.

God wants His people in the last days on earth to be simple and plain and clearly identifiable as His people in how they dress. He wants that difference to be there, not only to represent the natural simplicity and beauty He gave us all at Creation—but also to help "the world" to be able easily to pick us out of the crowd. God knew that when, through even how we dress, He could get the attention of unbelievers, they would take notice—and that would lead to saving encounters with His people.

Peter wrote:

> Do not let your adornment be merely outward—
> arranging the hair, wearing gold, or putting on fine
> apparel—rather let it be the hidden person of the heart,

with the incorruptible beauty of a gentle and quiet spirit, which is very precious in the sight of God. (1 Peter 3:3, 4)

Just as we must choose which is more important between flesh or spirit, we must also choose whether to focus on our "outer" or "inner" selves. In fact, these two sets of priorities are closely linked. When we focus our attention on adorning or decorating our outer person, that only builds selfishness—self-centeredness. And self is the essence of what it means to live in the "flesh."

God is so clear here! He wants us to concentrate on making ourselves beautiful on the inside. He wants us to develop characters of love and giving and service. And He knows that this is crucial if we are to carry out our last-day missions for Him.

Why? While jewelry, flashy clothing, and heavy facial makeup draw people to US, loving characters draw people to HIM! And only when people are drawn to Jesus can they be saved from certain eternal oblivion.

3. THE PRINCIPLE OF ECONOMY

To quote now more of Paul's verse in Principle #1:

...in like manner also, that the women adorn themselves in modest apparel, with propriety and moderation, not with braided hair or gold or pearls or costly clothing, but, which is proper for women professing godliness, with good works. (1 Timothy 2:9, 10)

Gold. Pearls. Costly clothing.

Now, is there something intrinsically unspiritual or even sinful about gold? Or pearls? Or even expensive clothing?

Is God anti-jewelry? If so, how does that square with the fact that He makes the main gate to the New Jerusalem out of one enormous pearl—paves the streets with solid gold, and makes the city gates out of precious stones?

Is God just trying to restrict our freedom as Satan has charged? Is He some great heavenly wet blanket insisting His followers wear drab clothing and forgo anything beautiful?

Someday, we will be walking those golden streets. We'll be surrounded by jewels, pearls, and incredible beauty. So why this requirement for the here and now, of leaving these things aside?

For one thing, we've already noted that while we're still here on earth with fallen, selfish human natures, we are just all too prone to "use" God's beautiful things to call attention to ourselves and reinforce our basic self-centeredness.

But there's another reason too. We are in special battlefield conditions right now. We need to be traveling light. Even in what we wear, we need to be keeping things simple. But we also need to be wholehearted in our commitment to helping win this final battle. And that means dedicating all our resources to that effort.

Not for a minute do I think that God is like an airline security agent, just waiting to catch us wearing something on the "No" list. God's concern is for not only the "calling attention to self" risk but also for the expense. It's so easy to channel enormous resources into things like jewelry and expensive clothing. Meanwhile, there is a world to reach and win—and to do that takes great resources. Resources that God has placed in the hands of His followers—to whom He has given the power to generate income and even wealth.

First Corinthians 10:31 says that we are to do everything to the glory of God. That includes how we dress. Just as the dress of a Special Forces soldier reflects on the commander in chief, the way God's Special Forces soldiers dress either gives Him honor—or does not.

In this final battle, we are a special, called-out people. "But ye are a chosen generation, a royal priesthood, an holy nation, a peculiar people; that ye should shew forth the praises of him who hath called you out of darkness into his marvellous light" (1 Peter 2:9).

A peculiar people. Not odd—but unique. Chosen. People who can be easily distinguished from those who aren't part of God's Special Forces, even in how they dress.

In Exodus 33:5, God said to the children of Israel, "Ye [are] a stiffnecked people: I will come up into the midst of thee in a moment, and consume thee: therefore now put off thy ornaments from thee, that I may know what to do unto thee."

Do you really think God did not know what to do with them? Remember, God sees the heart. He already knows us through and through. At this time God's so-called "special people" were too much into themselves, and they had started to become too much like the rest of the world. They had been called out of Egypt. They were specially chosen to be shining lights so that more people would come to the Lord. Since we cannot know for sure the heart, we have to be fruit inspectors. The people of this world have a right to look and see what makes us different.

Sometimes as Christians, we say we are shocked by how people in "the world" live. But that doesn't shock me. When people are without Jesus and just follow their sinful desires, how can we EXPECT them to act as God wants people to act?

What shocks me is that "the world" is not more shocked by how WE live! If we were really eating, dressing, and living as God outlines for us, the difference between "the world" and Christians would be dramatic—unmistakable. But when Christians look, act, and live the same—or nearly the same—as "the world," why should they be shocked?

When I suggest that it would be a good thing for the world to be shocked when they see Christians, I want to say that this would be a good thing because the difference would create curiosity. People of the world would be curious, not only about how we look and act on the outside—but also curious and even attracted by what shines forth from the inside!

If we were living as we should, we wouldn't need to spend so much time telling "the world" what we think it needs to know. We could, and should, talk less—and live more. Drawn by the way we live our lives, people who don't know Jesus will approach US—we won't need to approach THEM. They will ask us why we live the way we do, and especially, how we can be so happy and at peace, even though we look and act in such a "peculiar" way.

Should we be self-conscious about dressing plainly as God's last-day followers? Should we feel embarrassed because we don't wear what everyone else does? Should we feel put-upon by the requirements and restrictions of God's dress code for His elite troops?

Or should we not instead feel honored, privileged, and proud?

Stand tall, soldier! You serve the King of this universe!

THE BOTTOM LINE:

1. In this chapter, I gave several reasons that in the Rangers, we were proud of our uniforms. Are you proud of how God asks you to dress? Or do you feel odd, peculiar, self-conscious, or even ashamed?

2. What three Bible principles of dress were discussed in this chapter?

3. What happens when those in the world notice a great difference between themselves and true Christians?

CHAPTER TEN

Marked Men...
Marked Women

"**Y**ou can tell a lot about a person by . . ."

By what? Her hair? His shoes? How he or she acts in a crisis? How about by how a person speaks?

Have you ever tried to figure out what part of the country someone is from by how they speak? Of course, it's easy to spot a non-American accent, whether Spanish, French—even British English. But in the United States, all kinds of speech patterns exist.

Some examples:

New England: "He pahked his cah in the Hahvid yahd" ("He parked his car in the Harvard yard"). Or, "She caught a tuner off the coast of Cuber" ("She caught a tuna off the coast of Cuba").

Texas: "Fact of the bidness is, ya'll jess cain't unnerstand Tegs'n." ("The fact of the business is, you just can't understand Texan").

Minnesota: "You boyce go to Dooloot dere, you betcha" ("You boys go to Duluth, for sure").

New York City: "Aye—you want that I should getcha theh, oh what?" ("Hey, do you want me to get you there, or not?"...typical response of a New York cabbie when passenger protests about his hair-raising driving).

Teenager: "Like, he's da bomb—know what I'm sayin'?" ("He's a great guy").

Yes, *you can tell a lot about a person by his or her speech.* That was true in my Army and Special Forces training, too. Our drill instructors and trainers had their own vocabularies, believe me. A lot of what they had to say I can't repeat in this book. But take it from me—we got the point!

We recruits and soldiers also had our own "lingo"—a special informal vocabulary of words passed from one generation of trainees to another. For example:

▶ *Grunt*—an infantry soldier
▶ *Full bird*—a colonel
▶ *High and tight*—fresh haircut
▶ *Liberty*—time off
▶ *Head*—bathroom
▶ *PX*—post exchange (store)

Some of our military jargon, only those of us in the service would be likely to understand, but some of these terms distinguished us as part of the military when civilians heard us talking. They could tell we were soldiers just by how we spoke.

But it wasn't just our speech that marked us—other distinguishing marks too set us apart from those outside the military. When I finished my AIT (Advanced Individual Training) to become part of the 75th Ranger Regiment, I was issued a special shoulder insignia patch—to wear on my uniform.

Those who went on for even more advanced training in Ranger School were also issued the special embroidered "Ranger tab" to wear.

Rangers at that time also wore the distinctive black beret and other items of clothing that set them apart, not just from civilians, but even from the regular Army, as being a select and elite force of highly trained soldiers.

As Army Rangers, we could be distinguished in a number of ways:

▶ Our speech
▶ Our diet
▶ Our insignia
▶ Our uniforms
▶ Our mission
▶ Our specialized training
▶ Our level of commitment
▶ Our demeanor and behavior

If all these distinguishing marks were true for me as an Army Ranger, I can say with certainty that today that people can also tell I am a Christian by my distinguishing marks. And if you are a Christian, the world around you should also be able to *see* and *tell* and *know* that you are a Christian as they see these same distinguishing marks in you.

It reminds me of that old saying, "If you were brought to trial on charges of being a Christian, would there be enough evidence to convict you?" Something to think about!

When people look at you or me—when they hear us talk, see how we dress, how we eat, what we do for entertainment, how we behave even when we don't realize anyone is looking—what do they see? Do we stand out and apart from most people? Are we truly different? What kind of statement do we make to the world by our lives and how we live them? As we asked in the previous chapter, is the world shocked when they see how we look and how we live? Is it impossible for them not to see the great difference between us and those who do not follow Jesus?

"No man is an island, entire of itself," wrote the great poet John Donne. We are all interconnected in various ways here on this planet. With some, that connection is remote—but with some, it is close and profound. What I'm saying here is that, realize it or not, each of us has a great impact on those around us. Our influence is far greater than we imagine.

When we fail in our influence, it can turn people away from religion—from God. In the New Testament, even Peter failed one time by preaching one thing and living another, and Paul had to rebuke him.

It's important that if you are a Christian—and if I am—that we always stay aware of how our influence and example could be affecting others.

In earlier chapters, we looked at how God's Special Forces—His last-day elite soldiers in the war against evil—are special in every imaginable way. Let's review. Like Army Rangers, Navy SEALs, the Green Berets, and other elite military units, God's Special Forces . . .

▶ Are volunteers for special, sometimes dangerous missions.

▶ Undergo rigorous, intense special training.

▶ Become proficient in the use of specialized equipment and weapons.

▶ Develop strength and endurance through a special diet and fitness-training regimen.

▶ Wear special clothing suited to their mission.

Now, in this chapter, we've begun to focus on the importance of distinguishing marks—both for military Special Forces and for God's Special Forces. Some of those distinguishing marks, such as specialized diet and clothing, we've already discussed. So now, in addition to the area of speech mentioned early in this chapter, let's focus on how God's Special Forces can also be identified by how they live their daily lives.

RECREATION AND ENTERTAINMENT

Is there—or at least should there be—a difference between what most people in the world do for recreation and entertainment and what Christians do?

Only someone who just woke up from decades in a Rip Van Winkle–like coma would not be aware that society is engaged in a great war of cultural and moral values. And despite how politicians and the media make use of this intense struggle for their own self-interested purposes, it is real nonetheless.

Pardon me for wondering about something. If parents (some, at least) don't want to expose their children to the values routinely portrayed on TV and in the movies, why do they think those same values are OK for adults?

The Bible says, "Finally, brethren, whatever things are true, whatever things are noble, whatever things are just, whatever things are pure, whatever things are lovely, whatever things are of good report, if there is any virtue and if there is anything praiseworthy—meditate on these things" (Philippians 4:8).

True. Noble. Just. Pure. Lovely. Good. Virtuous. Praiseworthy.

Sound anything like the typical TV schedule or Hollywood movie? Hardly. Instead, the media serves up a steady diet of violence, lies, adultery, indecency, and every other vice that lurks in the dark corners of our human nature, and they call it entertainment. In addition, through its nonstop advertising, they seek to program our minds with values such as greed, envy, and pride—and to brainwash us (for that is what it is) with a set of life priorities that are anything but good and noble. Even the news these days is largely biased to the point of being little more than propaganda in some cases.

When I say that "the media" does this—meaning TV, radio, movies, print media, Internet advertising, and every possible cultural pipeline—yes, it's true that the media may be the channel. But the ultimate source of this tidal wave of negativity, filth and evil is Satan himself.

So God's chosen—His special last-day warriors—stand on the other side of the moral dividing line. They make a whole different set of choices when it comes to their leisure-time pursuits. For some, applying Philippians 4:8 means tossing out the TV altogether and avoiding not just theatrical movies that can't pass this scriptural standard but videos, DVDs, and other forms movies may take.

Other Christians may choose to carefully and even prayerfully select what movies they see—what TV programs they watch. And a valid point they make is that not everything is evil simply because it comes through media channels. That Satan uses the media does not mean he has a monopoly on it. The better impulses of human nature are creatively expressed too through dramas, documentaries, books, broadcasts, and music.

MUSIC

Music. Yes, this is another huge avenue through which the human mind and emotions and impulses can be reached. Music is one of the most powerful and universal of all human languages. And certain styles of music both create and reflect a certain mindset—a certain outlook on life. In recent years, some so-called "music" has become nothing but moral sewage. As I was growing up, rock and roll began. Today, even rock music looks tame.

Yet again, for Christians, there are choices. And true Christians can readily be distinguished—not only by their choices of leisure entertainment but also by their choices in music.

This is true even of the category known as "Christian" music.

In the wilderness, ancient Israel worshiped God with wonderful hymns and songs of praise and thankfulness.

But when Moses came down from Mount Sinai after forty days of communing with God and receiving the Ten Commandments, Joshua said to him (and I'm paraphrasing here—read the story in Exodus 32:17–19), "Do you hear that? From the noise coming from the camp, it's as if some kind of war is going on."

"No," Moses replied. "It doesn't sound to me like the shouts of either victory or defeat. It sounds like singing!"

Approaching the camp, Moses found that Aaron had given in to the people's demands for a golden calf to worship—they wanted their own idol-god, just like those of the heathen nations around them.

And now they were dancing, shouting, and singing with loud, frenzied music. The people were "running wild" and were "out of control," the New International Versions says (verse 24).

Even today, some so-called "Christian" music is little more than noise and commotion. Does it matter what kind of music we sing in church? If we are both influenced by music, and it reflects our inner thoughts and feelings, then yes, it matters a LOT!

In our current society, an entire lifestyle has developed—mostly among the impressionable young, but regrettably modeled too often by adults as well—that is fueled by illicit drugs and alcohol, combined with an anything-goes promiscuity, suggestive or even explicit music, and too much money and free time.

Young people choose as role models self-obsessed entertainers and sports "heroes," whose example of irresponsibility and indulgence and undeserved wealth these youth find enticing.

Even those of "a certain age" who should be well beyond such influences sweep up sensational tabloids in the supermarket lines to keep up with the latest gossip. Or these same adults become addicted to TV soap operas, "reality" shows, or explicit or violent programming. And even adults buy or download music that can't possibly elevate one's thoughts or refine one's life.

Christians, too, look at other leisure-time activities through the lens of their commitment to Christ and their special mission for Him in this world. So you can expect that a follower of Jesus will see some pursuits—gambling, dancing, and even becoming a serious fan of certain more violent sports, as examples—through different eyes than others would.

It's not my interest here to prescribe or get on my soapbox about every detail of how a Christian lives—what he or she chooses to do for recreation or entertainment. I am not the "Junior Holy Spirit"—my job is not to convict. That's the work of the Holy Spirit. I don't even think that prescribing or convicting should be the role of the church.

What I am interested in, though—and I think this is where the church too has a responsibility—is in reminding every Christian, first, of God's principles—His "better way." It's also my interest—and I hope that of the church—to remind people that they are called. They are chosen. They are special. They are unique. They are set apart by God for a special mission at the most critical time in all of earth's history. And that means that for those of us who follow our Master, life simply can't be "business as usual."

We can't waste our time, our resources, our minds, and morals, chasing after the bright lights and time-wasting preoccupations of the world around us. We are here for a reason—and that reason has to do with issues of life, death, and eternity.

Sometimes the world looks at Christians, and they shake their heads. Christians, they say, are totally negative. They are full of can'ts, don'ts, and shouldn'ts. Christians don't smoke. They don't drink. They don't do drugs. They don't sleep around. They don't live to eat—they eat to live. They don't dance. They don't gamble. They don't watch "bad" TV or movies. In other words, Christians are the biggest wet blankets on the planet. They don't believe in fun. They're against everything.

Unfortunately, that's too often *exactly* how people see Christians. We're the ones who can't and don't and are against everything fun. How utterly incredible! And how utterly wrong!

There are two ways we Christians can really "turn off" non-Christians. One is by keeping all the rules and laws—doing all the "do's" and not doing all the "don'ts"—yet looking clearly miserable because our hearts aren't in it. On the inside, we'd rather be doing just what "the world" is doing. In fact, we may feel a little deprived because we can't do what they do. We're legalists.

The other way our witness to the world goes nowhere is when we keep right on preaching the do's and don'ts—but we don't live them ourselves. The world is disgusted when Christians preach one thing and practice another. We're hypocrites.

And the world is "turned off" both by legalism and hypocrisy. But it will be irresistibly drawn to Christians who follow God's way of life AND are clearly happy, peaceful, and transformed by the Holy Spirit who lives in them.

KNOWN FOR WHAT WE'RE *AGAINST*?

We should be known for what we are *for*—not for what we are *against!* We should be the healthiest and happiest people wherever we work, wherever we live, wherever we mingle with those who don't know what we know . . . yet, anyway!

More flies can be caught with honey than with vinegar, they say. And if Christians run around with their faces all inverted like a prune as if they've just taken a huge swig of vinegar, something is wrong! If Christians look as if they're bearing the heaviest of crosses, and they go through life sighing and crying, something's wrong! Or if Christians go around with their noses in the air, filled with smug satisfaction that they don't do all the bad things other people do, something is really, really wrong!

Do you know why God chose the nation of Israel as His people in the Old Testament? He chose them to represent Him to the world around them. He wanted to demonstrate through them how awesome life can really be when people live by His natural and moral laws—how happy, healthy, and holy they could become by doing the exact opposite of what Satan led human beings to do.

But what happened? Tragically, Israel made three huge mistakes. First, they took all of God's principles and counsel, and made endless lists of hard-and-fast, rigid rules to keep. Instead of following God's way for the happy reward that was built into it, they followed His way instead from a sense of duty and obligation. They became fixated on laws, rules, penalties, and guilt.

Then they made a second great mistake. They became proud and self-satisfied with their efforts at law-keeping. They wanted nothing to do with the nations around them that were into sensuality, idolatry, and paganism. Why was this? Was it because they were not doing any of these things? No—a thousand times no! They were doing the very things the heathen were doing, but they were doing them in the name of the Lord. And because God called them to be a special people, to be a witness of His grace and mercy, they should have been more humble about that calling. It's so sad that they put themselves above the other nations. They truly believed they were better, when in reality, they were actually in many ways much worse. They held their religion in unrighteousness. They turned the "special" into the cursed.

And that mistake was linked to the third. The whole idea God had for choosing Israel was to show Himself and His ways to those very heathen people—*through Israel*. But ultimately, they failed in their assigned mission.

SHOWING BEATS TELLING

Here we are, just before Christ's second return to this earth to end the great war between good and evil. Once again, God has called out and chosen a special people—His last-day followers, His elite Special Forces. And He has again given them the same great mission: to tell the whole world the truth about God and His character of love. And not just to *tell* the world, but to *show* the world—to demonstrate the superiority of God's way by living it out right before the wondering eyes of those who don't yet know Him.

Yes, we are marked men and women. We can be distinguished

by how we live, by the choices we make, by how we spend our time and our resources, and by the values we hold high without compromise. We are marked to be seen as unique and "peculiar," so the world can see the difference between God's way and Satan's way.

Did you get that? Please don't miss that point. Our distinguishing marks—our vastly different lifestyle and set of values—is so that the world can see *the difference!* Because no greater difference exists in this universe than between God's values, His principles, His way of living—and Satan's.

Where Satan eagerly tries to sell the gratifications and short-term joys of selfishness, God is even more eager to demonstrate the benefits of love. Where Satan's way of life leads down a broad freeway to a cliff into the sea, God's more narrow way leads to an eternity of sinless joy and everlasting life.

We should never be ashamed to be different. It is an honor. It's a privilege. It's a calling. It's the highest mission to which anyone could ever aspire. Neither should we be proud in the sense of feeling superior to those who aren't "like us." All too often, that's how Christians appear to others—as exclusive, as self-righteous, as holier-than-thou. And it turns unbelievers off and away. But we can be proud in the good sense of feeling that we are engaged in something of indescribable importance. We can be proud that we represent the King of all that is true, good, and right.

There's a reason Uncle Sam calls his elite troops *Special* Forces. They truly are the few and the proud. Do those truly committed to being in the Special Forces complain about the things they *can't* do? Or are they more than happy to sacrifice some things in the service of a great cause and mission?

I remember to this day how I felt, dressed in my Army Ranger dress uniform: black beret, Ranger patch, special boots, creases sharp as razors, buckles shining mirror-bright. I knew I was somebody. I knew my mission was special. And I knew that my commitment mattered. Not once did I walk through an airport in my full-dress uniform and feel embarrassed or resentful.

Remind yourself right now: I'm part of the greatest military operation in all of human history—the final battle between good and evil. I'm called to surrender only what keeps me from accurately representing the King I serve. He only asks that I leave out of my life those things that would tear me down—that would undermine my body, mind, or spirit. I matter, because my King is depending on me. He needs me!

And He needs you too!

THE BOTTOM LINE:

1. What are some of the distinguishing marks of a Christian?

2. Do you think your church is known more for what it is FOR—or what it is AGAINST? Which, do you think, you might be most known for in the eyes of others?

3. Which is easier: telling people what God is like, or showing them?

CHAPTER ELEVEN

Warriors of Love

She was young and pretty—but nearly destitute. Times were hard, and the only job she could find was housekeeping. She didn't have the education to do much of anything else, and she detested her housekeeping work with a passionate intensity.

It was grinding, exhausting work. Scrubbing floors on hands and knees. Washing heavy pots and pans. Chopping wood for the cookstove. Laboring long, exhausting hours doing laundry on an old washboard. Yet, her wages were a stingy pittance—barely enough to buy a little food and a few necessities.

Worst of all, her employer was a tyrant. Nothing she did pleased him. The smallest mistake would send him into a towering rage. She had lost count of the times he had slapped and beaten her. It was little better than slavery, but being out of work would be even worse.

One morning, through no fault of her own, she arrived at work at 4:01 a.m.—one minute late. Her infuriated employer was waiting. He smothered her screams with one hand as he viciously pummeled her frail body with the other. After several long minutes, his rage spent, he carried her unconscious form outside and dropped her, face down, in the muddy street.

As she drifted slowly back to wakefulness, her eyes struggled to focus. She felt pain, fear, and bewilderment. Where was she? She could see clearly now but decided she must be dreaming. She lay on a luxurious canopied bed with gold bedposts. Expensive tapestries and paintings . . . a large chandelier . . . deep carpeting . . . velvet-upholstered furniture.

"What is your name, Miss?"

She shrank back in terror and surprise as she stared at the young man who had suddenly appeared in the doorway.

"It's all right," he assured her, noting her fright. "You're safe here. Now, come, tell me your name."

"I'm Heather," she replied. "Heather Hathaway."

"Happy to make your acquaintance, Heather," the young man replied. "I'm John Manchester."

Heather caught her breath. *John Manchester.* Everyone in town knew that John was the heir to one of the largest fortunes in the world. In fact, some said his father was the world's wealthiest man. Heather also knew that John was considered in upper social circles as one of the most eligible bachelors in the country.

"How did I get here?" she asked.

"I found you and brought you here," John explained. "Do you feel like telling me what happened?"

Tearfully, Heather recited the sad details of her plight. John listened attentively as she poured out her woe.

"Tell you what, Heather," John said when she had fully unburdened herself. "You stay right here in this guesthouse until you've recuperated a bit. I'll have a nurse look after you. Then, when you're feeling better, I could use a housekeeper for the main house up the hill from here, if you're interested. The work probably wouldn't be much different from what you've already been doing, but I'd be willing to pay you considerably more than that scoundrel who threw you out. And you could live here in the guesthouse. What do you say?"

Heather struggled to find words. "Yes. Yes, Sir! I'd like that very much!"

A few days later, Heather began her work in John Manchester's mansion. She found John as true as his word. Her wages were more than she'd ever made in her entire life. And her work was far less wearing. But she still detested her livelihood and hoped that someday she might do something else.

She scrubbed floors, washed pots and pans, and carried in wood for the cookstove, not because she enjoyed the work, but because of her generous pay and for fear of displeasing her new employer and losing this far better job.

As the weeks stretched into months, Heather became increasingly perplexed by John's actions. He had begun paying her far more attention than she would have thought a wealthy heir would pay a simple housekeeper. She couldn't understand it. And when he took her to an exclusive store in town and bought her clothes such as only the wives of rich men wore, she was flattered and exquisitely pleased but deeply puzzled. Why was he doing this?

Slowly it became obvious to her that, incredible as it seemed, John Manchester was falling in love with her. And as she fathomed this dizzying possibility, she began to realize something she had not permitted herself to admit: she had also fallen in love with him.

But future days proved that it was all very true.

At last came the unforgettable day when John asked Heather if she would become his wife. Their courtship was rapturous, the wedding transporting, the honeymoon heavenly.

John wanted very much to hire a new housekeeper. But Heather would have none of it. Nothing gave her greater pleasure than making a home for her beloved husband. It was amazing even to her that she should feel so differently now toward her work. She still washed dishes and scrubbed floors, though John insisted that she leave the heaviest work to someone else. But now she sang as she worked. What had been heavy drudgery was now a joy. She loved it.

There wasn't anything she wouldn't do for that man. Not anything.

In this short parable, Heather Hathaway knew what it was like to work as a slave, driven by duty and fear. She also discovered what it was like for her work to be motivated by love. She found the joy of doing all she could to please the one she loved.

God isn't looking for people who serve Him as slaves. He doesn't want His followers to keep His rules because they fear what He might do to them if they don't. He wants His followers to obey Him and keep His commandments and pay attention to His rules because they have responded to His love and have fallen in love with Him in return. Because He knows that if they love Him, they will just naturally be filled with a passionate desire to please Him. That's what love does.

In the Bible, God's people are called His bride—not His slaves. And when we come to love Him, doing His will changes from a reluctant or fear-driven duty to the highest privilege and joy.

In this book, I've shared a lot about the discipline and the demands of being part of God's last-day volunteer Special Forces. And believe me, that discipline—and those demands—are very real.

These are not normal times. And the task God has for us is not a routine assignment. We're at war—in fact, we're in the final battle of that war just before Jesus returns. And while His enemy tries to win the battle by lies and deception and promising the gratification of every selfish desire, Jesus fights back with love. Yes, in a very real sense, love is His most potent weapon. And ultimately, love will conquer and reign supreme in this universe.

So God needs warriors of love.

But how can any of us be effective members of God's final Special Forces if we're enlisted—but hating every minute of it? How can we win people by love if our own service for God is driven by duty? How can we be good soldiers for God if we detest His rules and requirements?

Yes, God does have rules and requirements. He knows that in this final military action against the invasion of selfishness that erupted long ago in His universe, no halfway measures will do. It will take extraordinary commitment, focused effort, and soldiers who are at their absolute best.

You and I can't be at our best if we are distracted by pursuing our own selfish wishes and choices. If we aren't willing to endure the discipline of training, aren't willing to sacrifice whatever would water down our efforts in the heat of battle, aren't willing to trust God's orders for us as our Commander—then our effectiveness for God will be hampered or even destroyed.

Does God ask us to dress a certain way? To eat a certain way? To choose what kinds of music we listen to? To use our resources of time and money in a certain way? To be seen as unique and distinctive by the world around us? You bet!

But is God asking all this of us to deprive us or because He demands we give things up for no good reason? Or is it that God knows not only that soldiers in a war need to travel light and be healthy, but that there's an even greater reason? You see, the enemy we battle is determined to destroy everyone around us—every last man, woman, and child on this planet.

There is only one hope for people to escape the enemy's destruction. They must be won over by the power of love—they must be confronted by the love of God and yield to it. That is their *only* hope!

THE FOCUS CAN'T EVER BE ON US!

And if we are to help God to reach the people around us, the focus must be on Him—not on us! Let me run that one past you again: As we present God's love to the people around us, the focus can't be on us—it must be on Him! In other words, He must increase—and we must decrease.

If people look at us, and all they see is a reflection of themselves, they won't be drawn to that. But if they look at us and see how different we are—how transformed our lives have become through the power of God's love—then they will pay attention!

So do we eat or dress differently than they do? Do they see a difference in what we do with our leisure time? Do they see a difference in our families? Our finances? Our health? Our level of happiness? Do we seem content while they feel empty?

Please, I beg you, my fellow volunteer in God's service, let's not resent how different God may ask us to be. Let's not chafe under His discipline. Let's realize that when we truly love God, we have something the entire world is desperately seeking but often not finding.

Satan, the enemy constantly hammers home his message that happiness is found in money, fame, power and control, sex without rules, self-indulgence, and "doing your own thing." And he's found a lot of buyers—even, and perhaps, among those who call themselves Christians—for what he's selling.

But one generation after another, young people who dream of wealth and fame and a world without rules find too late in life that the Devil's promise was an illusion. None of those roads lead to happiness. Quite the opposite—they lead to pain, emptiness, depression, and ruin.

Ask even those who amass great wealth if their riches have made them happy and fulfilled. Ask those whose names are known across the land if their fame brought them happiness and made them feel they really matter. Ask those who have lived only for pleasure if eating, drinking, and living as they pleased brought them peace inside or made them feel truly valued.

There's a whole world of people around us, desperately seeking happiness and peace, fulfillment, and just to feel special and loved.

I ask this most serious question: Do you realize what an awesome privilege it is that we are the ones with the map to where the treasure is? We are the ones who can feed this world's ravenous hunger for real love—not just the devil's cheap imitations? We, too, may have begun as beggars, but we have found the Bread of Life—and it's our mission and privilege to tell others where it is!

When you woke up this morning, you were in a war zone—the war between Satan's lies and God's truth, between his empty "promises" and God's reality, between ultimate tragedy and death and everlasting life and joy.

And if a major part of how God plans to press the battle today against selfishness is through volunteers in His Special Forces—volunteers who will be channels for His love and truth to a desperate and dying world—then we don't want to let Him down.

Because someone today may be drawn by how we live our life to the Commander we trust and obey. Someone sick of sin may see our peace and happiness and want what we have. Someone may notice that we are "different" and see in that difference what they've spent their entire lives trying to find.

Could the stakes be any higher?

As we move through this day, we will either be in the service of the enemy (whether by choice or default)—or in the service of God. And if you and I choose to be in His service, why not go "all in"? Why hold anything back? Why not make a total commitment? Why not sell out to God?

THE BOTTOM LINE:

1. Why and how is love the only antidote for legalism?

2. Do you ever resent that God asks you to be so different from the world?

3. Do you realize just how closely others watch the sermon you're preaching with your life?

✪ CHAPTER TWELVE ✪

Classified Intelligence Report

> NOTICE: This chapter contains top-secret intelligence exposing the tactics, strategies, and goals of the enemy. It takes you behind enemy lines.

I really do want you to read this whole book because all of it is important. But this chapter isn't just important—it's *life-and-death* important. It's indispensable, vital, crucial.

Why? Because in this chapter, it's my privilege to share with you WHY it's so important to be part of God's Special Forces. In fact, I'm going to share something personal with you right now.

When this book was all written and ready to be printed, I sat down with the manuscript one last time to read it again. When I did, I had a restless feeling, and the question kept coming to my mind, "What's missing?" Finally, it came to me. I needed to focus more forcefully on WHY being in God's last-day Special Forces is so significant.

And here is the answer: We must have a CAUSE—a motivating, powerful cause that's more important than *anything* to us—more important than our personal comfort and ease, more important than our name or reputation, more important than succeeding at our goals, more important than any of our human relationships, more important than even our lives!

In the Army Special Forces, I can tell you that I definitely had a cause. Yes, there were some personal reasons that drove me to join the military—reasons I share elsewhere in this book: the desire to matter, to be somebody, to "be all that I could be."

But, I also wanted to be part of something bigger than myself. I wanted to make a difference with my life, beyond my own personal goals and dreams. And in the Army, I found that cause. I was part of my country's first line of defense. I was standing on the wall of defense to drive back any evil forces that would attack or threaten my nation. I helped make sure that my fellow Americans could sleep well at night, knowing that their freedom was being protected.

And I'll tell you something: that felt good!

In time, though, my military service had ended, and as I launched into life, I still had a hunger deep inside to matter—to do something special with my life. In my book *Learning to Walk With God*, I've shared the story of my life in full, but let me refer to a part of it briefly now.

After my years in the Army, I began to live what many would call the "American Dream." I married a wonderful woman, we had three beautiful children, I became very successful in business and began making a lot of money...but...

Inside, I knew I was still missing something.

A time came when we attended a series of meetings at a church, and even though I'd heard previously many things the preacher presented, God spoke to my heart in a new and powerful way. He knew the many questions that tumbled over each other in my mind:

▶ Why so many divorces? How can so many marriages that began with—"For better or for worse, for richer, for poorer, in sickness and in health, to love and to cherish from this day forward, until death do us part"—end up in total disaster?

▶ Why so much violence in the world and such an obsession with making money? Why so many rapes, child kidnappings, and murders so terrible that it is not even good to talk about them?

▶ Why so many churches that claim to go by the Bible, yet they are so different?

▶ Why are countries still fighting each other?

If only I could answer these questions, I knew the "how" would become easier. The Bible says there is a reason for everything under the sun.

I heard God's voice speaking to me inside. It's as if He said, "Dwight, you can help Me put a stop to all this. You can help me tell other people what is going on behind the scenes in this world. Let Me reveal the answers to you through My Word and then train you. I will let you see what is going on behind the scenes. I will help you uncover Satan's plan. If you will hang in there and are willing to be made willing, then you will be a part of the greatest cause you've ever known."

In my mind and my heart I said to the Lord, "By your Grace, I will learn of You. I give You my whole heart today. Teach me, and show me the truth."

I've always loved people, and God's voice speaking to me directly really touched my heart—so I was more than ready to answer God's call.

I began to immerse myself in the Word of God.

Little by little, I began to see how the Devil had pulled the wool over the eyes of most of the world—how he had deceived, distracted, and fooled people. My eyes seemed to open, and I began to see *why* the world around me was in such a mess. The Devil had even pulled the wool over the eyes of many good Christians. The fog started to lift, and I could see why Christians, including myself, had and are being hoodwinked by Satan.

But at this major turning point in my life, I also began to see that the world around me needed to understand that being a Christian—following Jesus—was more than accepting that He had died on the Cross for them, as wonderful as that is. I realized that not only has Jesus done something amazing FOR us all, He also wants to do something THROUGH us!

I could see that Jesus is urgently looking for people through whom He can live out His life—so that they reflect His very own character to the world around them. As I studied and thought about it more, it became so clear to me. In John 14:6, the Bible says, "I am the Way, the Truth, and the Life." Because God loves us so much, He does give us freedom to choose. He knows what the Devil is planning and how he will deceive the whole world by making the package look so good on the outside; yet, when it is unwrapped, garbage is found inside the package.

It reminds me of a perfectly good egg I was going to use to make a cheese omelet. The sad thing about the so-called perfectly good egg was that it was rotten when I cracked it open, and the smell almost turned my stomach. It was just plain nasty!

Many things of this world look good, until we see them for what they really are. This is the reason Jesus hasn't come back even though 2,000 years have passed since He returned to heaven. He is waiting for a special people—a group of those who will follow Him wherever He leads, no matter where it is or how hard it seems—to adopt His cause.

THE BREATHTAKING CAUSE!

Inside, I knew I wanted desperately to be one of those people. I'd always wanted to be someone as fully surrendered to God as were Elijah or Enoch in the Old Testament. Before this, I had wanted to be such a man for God, now I saw *why!* There was a cause so great that it took my breath away.

That cause was—and is—to tell the truth to the world both about God and about His enemy, Satan. That cause opens people's eyes to the fact that behind all the busyness of their daily lives, and behind all the headlines they read or newscasts they watch, something huge is going on that's bigger than they realize.

An enormous, life-and-death battle is being fought on between good and evil in this universe—a great conflict or controversy between Christ and Satan. And that war affects everything that's happening here on this earth. It affects every nation, every event, and every person. It affects you and me. *And almost no one knows the truth of what's really happening!* It's not because you and I aren't smart enough to know—it's because so few of us read the Scriptures for what they say. In fact, most of us hardly read them at all. I just talked with a pastor who shared with me that before he gave his heart to the Lord, he knew nothing at all about the Bible. He had gone to church when he was young, but he couldn't even remember one text in the Bible.

"I knew all the football and hockey players by name, though. I knew their statistics, their ages, where they grew up, if they were married, and how much they made. When I look back now, it thoroughly embarrasses me! Here I knew all these things that not only took a lot of time to research and memorize, but when I became totally honest with myself, I came to the stark realization that the only thing it did for me was to puff myself up to my friends. It was as if to tell them, 'Hey guys, look at me—look how much I know! Aren't I cool?' Big Deal. Yet, something that would make a difference for an eternity I knew nothing about. How sad! When I began to see and understand this, I knew that I had found the cause of my life—the very reason I'm even here."

When we embrace the cause, many lost and miserable people in this world find great relief from their sins and guilt when they realize that Jesus died on the Cross to save them from death. But few realize that Jesus wants not just to deliver us from sin's *penalty* but also from its *power*—it's an addictive hold over our lives. So many, even good Christians, accept Jesus as their Savior from sin's penalty based on what He's done on the Cross. But how many even realize that He also wants them to accept Him as their Lord, so He can also save them from having to just go on sinning?

Getting Only Half the Good News

It's as if the world often is getting only *half* of the Good News! That is why most Christians have the same failure rate that the people outside the church have.

What God wants—what He's looking for today—is a group of people who will follow Him so fully that they let Him change them from the inside out. And that can only happen when people—and I'm talking about you and me—allow Jesus to come into their hearts to be Lord and Master when we let Him live out His life in and through us. "I have been crucified with Christ," Paul wrote. "It is no longer I who live, but Christ lives in me" (Galatians 2:20).

As I learned more about this great cause to which I knew God was calling me, I also found that the more I know Jesus, the more I love and trust Him. And that is what Jesus needs today—people who will love Him so much that they "trust and obey" Him.

Remember Abraham in the Bible? That whole story is found in Genesis 22. God asked Him to do something that seemed impossible—insane, even. He asked Abraham to take his only son Isaac to the mountaintop and sacrifice him on an altar. Can you even imagine how you'd feel in the same situation? To take your only son—the one who was supposed to have sons and daughters as the sands of the seas—and sacrifice him? And it was not just killing his own son, but the way in which he had to kill him—as a burnt-offering sacrifice.

You can find out how you'd have done a burnt offering to the Lord—had you lived in Old Testament times (Leviticus 1:4-9).

First, of course, you had to kill the offering. Next, you took the blood and sprinkled it around the altar. Dads and moms, think of this: How could you even think of killing one of your children anyway? But to kill your only son and then sprinkle his blood on an altar is almost overwhelming. I wish I could say it would stop there, but it would only be getting started.

Next, you would have to skin and cut the body in pieces. Wow! After this, you would lay the parts of the body in order—the head and the fat on the wood. Finally, you would wash the entrails and the legs with water. And after all this was completed, you would burn the offering.

Can you even begin to comprehend the thoughts Abraham might have had? The Bible says he left very early in the morning. I am sure he never told his wife or even the servants who stayed at the camp. With a heavy heart, he started on his mind-crushing journey.

I know that when there is something I just don't want to do, I want to just get done with it. Abraham had to walk with his son and two servants for three days. He would for sure have liked to talk to someone about it, but he couldn't. They would have thought he was crazy. They would have tried to stop him. He had to keep it all between him and his God. Not even his son knew what God had asked of his father.

Did Abraham protest, "I must be imagining things. And if I'm not—if You really are asking me to kill my only son, then what kind of God are You? No, now You've gone too far"?

No, Abraham trusted and obeyed God completely. He took Isaac to the mountaintop, built the altar, and raised his knife to slay his only son. Only then did God stay his hand. What God wanted Abraham to know was, would he trust Him, no matter what? Did Abraham love and trust Him enough to pay any price? Do you see? Abraham knew his Father's voice because he had made it a habit to be in the Word and learn to obey it, because of his love. In other words, he knew his Father's voice. He also trusted God so much that he knew God could raise Isaac from the ashes if need be. Do you see that when the price was high enough, the how became easier?

And what about Job? The Devil took away his family, his wealth—

everything. His friends told him that God hated him because he was such a sinner. His wife told him to curse God and die. But Job said, "Though he slay me, yet will I trust in him" (Job 13:15).

And nearer to our time, what about John Bunyan? He is the author of one of the top-ten best-selling books of all time: *Pilgrim's Progress*.

After John was converted, he began to preach wherever he could draw a crowd. But preaching in public was illegal. So he was threatened with prison if he didn't stop. John Bunyan kept right on preaching, and before long, he was thrown in jail.

Several years passed, and he was given a choice. If he'd promise never to preach again, he could be free. You know what he said? "If I was out of prison today, I would preach the gospel again tomorrow, by the help of God."

Would we do the same? Does Jesus mean enough to us that we'd do *anything at all* for Him? Would we tell the world the truth about Him? And about His great enemy?

At the beginning of this chapter is a notice that this chapter contains top-secret intelligence about Satan. It reveals what he's really trying to accomplish in this world and in your life and mine. And in the following chapter, I want to spend a few moments sharing some of what the Devil is doing—and how he's doing it. After that, I want to share something far more powerful and important: what Jesus is doing!

THE BOTTOM LINE:

1. What was the overriding CAUSE of my life that I discovered and shared in this chapter?

2. One-half of the Good News is that Jesus is our Savior. What is the other half?

3. Have you arrived at the place in your relationship with Jesus that you are willing to do *anything at all* for Him?

CHAPTER THIRTEEN

Selling Out to God

One of the primary rules for success in any battle—whether it's a military or spiritual one—is this: "Know your enemy." If you don't know your enemy's tactics, plans, and strategies, you will most certainly be defeated. So it's vital that we learn all about Satan's tactics, and what he is doing to try and destroy us.

When Satan rebelled against God, he came up with what he thought was a very creative way to get himself "off the hook," so to speak, in the eyes of the rest of the universe—the unfallen angels who wouldn't join him in his rebellion, and the unfallen inhabitants of other worlds. Here's what he might have said, not only in his mind, but also to the other angels:

> "God made a law that restricts us, and we are not really free. It's unfair. It's impossible for anyone ultimately to be free, and at the same time, have to keep this so-called law of liberty. God said we are free to do what we want, but I don't think we are because we have this set of rules dangling around our necks ready to hang us anytime we think differently than God. I can see that we could do much better if we could do a few things a little—and I mean just a little—differently.

I will give you just one example, my loyal angels. I think if we change the music just a little, we could and would have more exciting worship to our Lord. I am the leader of our great heavenly choir, you know, and I do have some experience in this.

This is maybe a slightly simplistic illustration, but do you see what began to happen to Satan when he started to lose his trust in God? We know that God suffered long with Lucifer. I am sure that God tried to appeal to him many times to let it go—to trust in the One who was all-knowing. But at the end of every conversation, God let Lucifer make the final choice.

That is the freedom our heavenly Father has allowed each of us to exercise. We are always free to make choices. Sometimes we forget that with those choices inevitably come consequences. Depending on the choice we make, those consequences are sometimes—in the worst-case scenario—life-threatening.

That is what happened to Satan. He made choices that got him and a third of the angelic host kicked out of heaven. What a sad consequence for such a heavenly being! I wish the story would have ended there, but as most of us know, it didn't. Satan could not let well enough alone. He figured that if he was lost, then as far as he was concerned, he would take down anyone he could. And he certainly was not going to play fair. He would be the best deceiver in the universe.

"I will get them to lose their faith and especially their trust in God," he told himself. "I will do this by painting a completely different picture of God—who He is, and what He is like—than they have ever seen. I'll get them to question whether He is really the same person they've always thought He is."[1]

Satan didn't want the angels to see God as He really is, and he doesn't want anyone today to see what God is really like. He doesn't want them to see God's character as loving and merciful and compassionate. Instead, he leads people to see God as angry, judgmental, and condemning—as doing all He can to make it hard to get into heaven.

How does Satan go about doing all this? First of all, he makes his appeal using a lie—a counterfeit—for every one of God's truths. Is God the Creator of heaven and earth? Then Satan will make believing in creation seem hopelessly simple-minded—and evolution seem intelligent and respectable. Does God believe in the home and marriage and the family? Then Satan will attack these gifts of God with all he has, making a game and mockery of marriage, tearing the family apart, and dragging sex into the gutter.

But Satan works not only through counterfeits but also through distractions: celebrity worship, TV viewing, sports obsessions, video games, and every conceivable form of entertainment. He also keeps millions focused mainly on their relationships— looking for "love" that's been diluted to "hooking up" and frantic text messaging and "hanging out" on Internet social sites.

He also works through addictions: alcohol, narcotics, sex, gambling, compulsive overeating, workaholism, and so many more.

All Satan really needs to do is keep people so preoccupied and busy with their work, their problems, their false beliefs, their addictions, and their distractions, that they have *no time* to know the truth about Jesus.

Let's look at a little clip of what I believe is happening behind the scenes. I can hear Satan saying this to his staff of evil angels:

"Listen up now. I have been thinking about this for thousands of years," Satan tells them, "and I have developed a most successful plan of causing these stupid humans to lose eternal life.

"The popular churches are already lulled to sleep by our deceptive power. By pleasing sophistry and lying wonders, we can continue to hold them under my control. Since these churches are already in our hands, we need to lay our snares especially for those who are looking for the second advent of Christ and endeavoring to keep all the commandments of God.

"We must watch those who are calling the attention of the

people to see the claims of the law of God. Let's keep the minds of these people in darkness until that work is ended, and we will secure the world, along with the church.

"We have caused worldliness to infiltrate the members of many churches. Now the church must be led to unite with the world in its support. We must work by signs and wonders to blind their eyes to the truth and lead them to lay aside reason and the fear of God so they will follow custom and tradition.

"I will influence popular ministers to turn the attention of their hearers from the commandments of God. That which the Scriptures declare to be a perfect law of liberty, we need to represent as a yoke of bondage. The people accept their minister's explanations of Scripture and do not investigate for themselves. Therefore, by working through the ministers, we can control the people according to our will.

"But our principal concern is to silence this sect of so-called 'special people'—the ones who seem to be totally surrendered to God. We must excite popular indignation against them. We will enlist great men and worldly men upon our side and induce those in authority to carry out our purposes. Then the counterfeit law that I have set up will be enforced by laws that are most severe and exacting. Those who disregard them will be driven from the cities and villages and made to suffer hunger and privation.

"Once we have the power, we will show what we can do with those who will not swerve from their allegiance to God. We led the Romish church 700 years ago to inflict imprisonment, torture, and death upon those who refused to yield to her decrees. Now that we are bringing the Protestant churches and the world into harmony with this right arm of our strength, we will finally have a law to exterminate all who will not submit to our authority. When death is made the penalty for violating my law, then many who are now ranked with commandment keepers will come over to our side.

"But before proceeding to these extreme measures, we must exert all our wisdom and subtlety to deceive and ensnare those who honor God's law. We can separate many from Christ by worldliness, lust, and pride. They may think themselves safe because they believe the truth, but indulgence of appetite or the lower passions, which will confuse judgment and destroy discrimination, will cause their fall.

"So go, make the possessors of lands and money drunk with the cares of this life. Present the world before them in its most attractive light that they may lay up their treasure here and fix their affections upon earthly things. We must do our utmost to prevent those who labor in God's cause from obtaining means to use against us. Keep the money within our own ranks. The more means they obtain, the more they will injure our kingdom by taking from us our subjects. Make them care more for money than for the upbuilding of Christ's kingdom and the spread of the truths we hate. We need not fear their influence, for we know that every selfish, covetous person will fall under our power and will finally be separated from God's people.

"Through those that have a form of godliness but know not the power of it, we can gain many who would otherwise do us harm. Lovers of pleasure more than lovers of God will be our most effective helpers. Those of this class who are apt and intelligent will serve as decoys to draw others into our snares. Many will not fear their influence because they profess the same faith. We will lead them to conclude that the requirements of Christ are less strict than they once believed, and that by conformity to the world, they would exert a greater influence with people that are not now in any church. Thus, they will separate from Christ, and then they will have no strength to resist our power, and before long, they will be ready to ridicule their former zeal and devotion.

"Until the great decisive blow shall be struck, our efforts against commandment keepers must be untiring. We must be present at all their gatherings. In their large meetings especially, our cause will suffer much, and we must exercise great vigilance and employ all our seductive arts to prevent souls from hearing the truth and becoming impressed by it.

"I will have upon the ground, as my agents, men holding false doctrines mingled with just enough truth to deceive souls. I will also have unbelieving ones present who will express doubts in regard to the Lord's messages of warning to His church. Should the people read and believe these admonitions, we could have little hope of overcoming them. But if we can divert their attention from these warnings, they will remain ignorant of our power and cunning, and we shall secure them in our ranks at last. God will not permit His words to be slighted with impunity. If we can keep souls deceived for a time, God's mercy will be withdrawn, and He will give them up to our full control.

"We must cause distraction and division. We must destroy their anxiety for their own souls and lead them to criticize, to judge, and to accuse and condemn one another, and to cherish selfishness and enmity. For these sins, God banished us from His presence; and all who follow our example will meet a similar fate."[2]

And meanwhile, as Satan and his deputies lay their detailed plans against God and His people, time on this earth is running out! People are dying every day who don't know Jesus. People are in darkest ignorance about the great war that is occurring over their own souls. They don't realize that both Satan and Jesus are trying to win their allegiance and loyalty.

Our great cause, as members of God's Special Forces, is to commit our lives to the great mission of pulling back the curtain so people can see what's really transpiring behind the scenes. It's our cause to tell the truth—both about God and His character, and Satan and his character. It's our cause to let people know that to follow Jesus, they must actively choose Him; all they have to do to belong to Satan is just do nothing—just floating and going with the flow. To make no choice is really to choose the enemy.

Please don't let Satan's tactics and strategies tear you away from the great cause to which God is calling you. Don't let Satan distract or discourage you. Don't let him tell you that you are too weak to overcome your bad habits—that you can never change—that you're not special.

There's some truth to that, of course. You can't change. And neither can I. But *living in us, Jesus can change us!* Nothing is too hard for Him. Nothing is impossible!

And that brings me to the place where I want to pull your attention away from Satan and his devices to Jesus and His power. I want you to see that part of joining His great cause is to help Him prove Satan's original charge to be completely false—the charge that God's law is too hard to keep.

Ever since Adam and Eve fell into sin, we've all been weak and sinful. How can we ever possibly obey God perfectly?

The good news is that we don't have to! But here's even better news: if we let Jesus come into our hearts and lives, He will live through us His own perfect life. Remember that verse? "Christ lives in me." It's found in Galatians 2:20.

How Do We Win People to Jesus?

Now, just how do we win people to Jesus as soldiers in His Special Forces? There are really two ways. First, God gives each of us talents and gifts. Some of us are more outgoing, some less so. Some of us can speak to others readily; some of us are timid. Some can preach, write, or give Bible studies; some share their skills or show hospitality.

One thing we all can do: we can ask Jesus every new morning to come into us, to live His life through us. We can ask Him to put us into contact during the day with people who need Him. When we do that, it's amazing the unexpected "divine appointments" God reserves just for us. When those happen, we have unplanned chances to share what Jesus has done for us—what He means to us.

So some of us can actively witness about Jesus to others: preaching, giving Bible studies, or teaching classes. But all of us can make ourselves available for Jesus to use each day as we meet family, friends, neighbors, coworkers, and even strangers.

There's one final way all of us can tell the truth about God.

Because, you see, when Jesus lives out His life through us—and it's no longer we who live but He who lives in us—people will see His character. They will see the love of Jesus flowing through our lives. They will see truth, compassion, acceptance, and mercy. When they see us, they may see our faces or our hands. When they hear us, it's our voices they hear. But really, it's Jesus reflecting from our faces. It's Jesus communicating His love through the gentle touch of our hands. It's the kindness of Jesus people are hearing in our voices.

It's really true: people are far more drawn to Jesus by how we live—by our characters—than by anything we preach, teach, or say.

To be part of God's Special Forces is to be committed to the greatest cause in all history—the chance to expose Satan and reveal Jesus! I can't begin to tell you how all-consuming my own desire is to continue committing my life to that cause. And I wish I had the tongues and the words of a million angels to help persuade you to be part of it too!

Won't you join me? Won't you sell out to Jesus with me? Won't you do whatever it takes, pay whatever the price, to be part of something bigger than all the universe—and as lasting as eternity? Won't you not only let the Cross of Jesus save you and break your sinful heart but also let the Jesus of that Cross live out His life in you now?

The clock is ticking. It's ticking on this earth—time is fast running out. It's ticking on Satan—thankfully, his days are numbered. It's ticking on your life and mine—what do you have left, 40, 30, 20, 10 years or so, if some sudden accident doesn't change that? The clock is ticking on people by the billions who are lost and in slavery to sin and Satan—people who are desperate for peace inside even as they chase it in pleasure-seeking, money-making, entertainment, or becoming more powerful.

The clock is ticking. Only a little time is left.

Have you made your own decision to join God's Special Forces?

If not, please choose what I have. You'll be grateful forever!

THE BOTTOM LINE:

1. Knowing Jesus is the path to eternal life, but why is it important that we also know our enemy?

2. What new insight did you gain from reading the extended "behind-the-scenes" look at Satan's planning in this chapter?

3. To you personally, what does it mean to "sell out to God"?

[1]Adapted from the chapter entitled "Snares of Satan" in the book Testimonies to Ministers.
[2]Adapted from the chapter entitled "Snares of Satan" in the book Testimonies to Ministers.